F O C U S   O N

Defence

Master Point Press
22 Lower Village Gate
Toronto, ON
M5P 3L7
(416) 932-9766
www.pathcom.com/~raylee

Distributors:

In Canada: Hushion House 1-800-263-4374
In U.S.A.: Barricade Books 1-800-59-BOOKS

Canadian Cataloguing In Publication Data
Roth, D.L.M. (Danny L.M.)
Focus on Defence
ISBN 0-9698461-4-2
1. Contract Bridge — Defensive play I. Title
GV1282.42.R68 1997   795.41'53   C97–931617-0

Cover and interior design: Zena Denchik
Editor: Ray Lee
Additional Analysis: Colin Lee

Printed and bound in Canada
2 3 4 5 6 7   03 02 01 00 99 98

FOCUS ON

Defence

DANNY ROTH

MASTER POINT PRESS

Foreword

In a companion book, *Focus on Declarer Play,* we looked at errors to avoid if you want to improve your dummy play. This book is, of course, twice as important! Unless your style of bidding is very selfish and/or competitive, you will, over a long period, defend twice as many hands as you declare and therefore proficiency in this area is twice as essential to your success in tournaments.

Common defensive mistakes can be divided into a number of categories of which the most important are probably the following:

1) Undue haste
The issue here is rushing to take, or to try to take, your tricks too quickly. To be fair, at matchpoints, it is often important to cash top tricks early for fear of conceding unnecessary overtricks but, even here, defenders must choose their moment; holding back is often a winning policy, at least in the long term.

2) Communications issues
Too many defences founder owing to failure to secure the defenders' lines of communication or to disrupt declarer's.

3) Ignoring available information
Defenders often fail to note and use information from the bidding and early play to place outstanding high cards and end up following lines of defence inconsistent with the picture on view.

4) Trouble with trumps
Trumps are a fascinating aspect of bridge, and it is vital to know how to make the most of the defenders' trump holdings.

5) Careless discarding
This is often the result of defenders, with very poor hands, losing interest in the proceedings. If your standard of card-holding is comparable to mine this could be a very expensive habit. A whole book could be written on this subject alone.

Contents

Undue Haste

1

The Bronze
Position

Followers of the Olympic Games and similar events will immediately connect the word 'bronze' with the competitor in third place. At bridge, once the opening lead has been faced and dummy tabled, it will be the duty of the 'third-place' defender in the East position (following the usual custom of calling declarer South) to plan the defence. Countless contracts are handed to declarer by thoughtless play at this point.

Third hand think!

If you are going to be a successful bridge player, your first priority is to remove beginners' parrot rules completely from your mind. The 'third-hand-high' rule, for example, should be regarded with the height of suspicion and this particularly applies when the card you are going to play is not all that high anyway.

Mistakes in this area can often be avoided if you consider the basic reason for playing third-hand-high. Usually, you will be hoping to win the trick outright or to knock out a high card from declarer in order to promote a trick for the defenders. If it is clear that neither applies, then it may well be wrong to dive in head first.

Strangely, while I was in the process writing this chapter, I watched two hands come up, within a quarter-of-an-hour of each other, where West had to sit helplessly as his partner cruelly swung the axe.

Dealer East
Both vulnerable

W	N	E	S
		pass	2NT[1]
pass	4NT	pass	6NT

[1] 20-22 points

North
♠ Q 10 8 4
♥ K 9 7
♦ A 10 2
♣ K 7 4

East
♠ K 7 5 3
♥ 6 5 3 2
♦ 7 5 4
♣ 6 3

Partner leads the ♠6 and dummy plays low. Which card do you play, and would it make any difference if declarer had called for the ♠Q?

This is the kind of situation where parrot rules lay out the surest route to disaster. What is the spade situation? Clearly, South has the ♠A — who is underleading an ace against a slam when sitting over a 2NT opener? Once you have established this, you are well on the way to finding the correct defence. If South has four spades, your king is dead, regardless of your defence. If he has fewer, the ace will drop in three rounds while your king remains intact so that declarer will make three rather than four spade tricks — all the difference in the world.

North
♠ Q 10 8 4
♥ K 9 7
♦ A 10 2
♣ K 7 4

West
♠ 6 2
♥ 10 8 4
♦ J 8 6 3
♣ Q 10 9 5

East
♠ K 7 5 3
♥ 6 5 3 2
♦ 7 5 4
♣ 6 3

South
♠ A J 9
♥ A Q J
♦ K Q 9
♣ A J 8 2

South is left with eleven tricks and no realistic play for the twelfth; third-hand-high gives him the slam. This applies irrespective of which card is played from dummy at trick one. But suppose dummy plays the queen and partner has the jack; should you not cover then? The answer is that this is simply not on. Firstly, jack to three is a bad lead in this kind of situation — likely, as here, to pick up anything in your hand. Secondly, put yourself in declarer's position. With ace doubleton or trebleton opposite that dummy, would you rise with queen? Who is leading away from a king against a slam when sitting well-placed over a 2NT opener?

Points to remember

1. Before playing third-hand high, consider why you are doing so.
2. Make an effort to place the remaining cards in the suit so that they are consistent with the bidding and play so far and only then decide whether 'third-hand-high' makes any sense.

The king can wait!

The unhappy West player in the first example was still nursing his
wounds when, just a couple of rounds later, a new pair arrived.

Dealer South   **North**
E-W vulnerable   ♠ 10 9 4 3

W	N	E	S
			1♥
pass	2♥	pass	3♦¹
pass	4♥		

♥ Q 9 8 4

♦ A 10 9

♣ J 7

¹ help-suit game try

                                       East

                                       ♠ K 8 7 6

                                       ♥ 7 6

                                       ♦ Q 7 5

                                       ♣ A 9 6 3

West leads the ♠5 and dummy plays low. Which card do you play
and would it make any difference if declarer had called for the ♠10?

That five certainly looks like a low card, suggesting an honour in partner's hand. Rising with the king, therefore, appears right, attempting to promote that honour. That, however, is only an initial prognosis. Careful examination of the spade pips reveals a different picture. If partner, indeed, has a trebleton honour, what is his holding? All the pips higher than the five are visible so this scenario becomes impossible. West must have a doubleton or singleton. Now rising with the king, regardless of dummy's card, is obviously fatal.

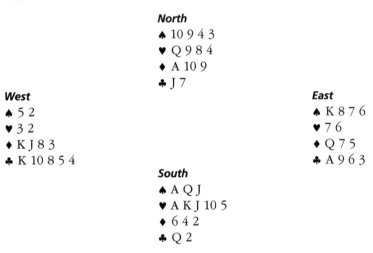

North
♠ 10 9 4 3
♥ Q 9 8 4
♦ A 10 9
♣ J 7

West
♠ 5 2
♥ 3 2
♦ K J 8 3
♣ K 10 8 5 4

East
♠ K 8 7 6
♥ 7 6
♦ Q 7 5
♣ A 9 6 3

South
♠ A Q J
♥ A K J 10 5
♦ 6 4 2
♣ Q 2

If East plays his king at trick one, declarer will take four spade tricks instead of his entitlement of three. Play low at trick one, however, and he is left with four unavoidable losers in the minors.

Points to remember

1. Do not jump to conclusions on the initial lead without careful consideration of the evidence. Far too many errors are made because players draw a dogmatic line, at about the six-spot, between 'high' and 'low'. An eight is low in 10 9 8; a five is high in 5 4 3 2. This point is particularly important in the world of suit-preference signalling.

2. You will have seen, in these two hands, that covering an honour with an honour is not necessarily right. It should only be considered when there is a significant chance of promoting a card in a defender's hand; otherwise it may well help, rather than hinder declarer.

Cherish your entry!

Having seen the idea, try this next example; again the same player sat as a heart-broken West, this time in a teams' event with IMP scoring.

| **Dealer South** | | | | **North** |
| **E-W vulnerable** | | | | ♠ K 10 9 |

W	N	E	S
			2NT[1]
pass	3NT		

[1] 20-22 points

North
♠ K 10 9
♥ 8 7 6
♦ K J 10 5 4
♣ 10 6

East
♠ 8 3 2
♥ 10 9
♦ 6 3 2
♣ J 7 5 3 2

Partner leads the ♣8 and dummy plays low. Which card do you play, and would it make any difference if declarer had called for the ♣10?

With any luck, you have been cured by now. What is the club situation? If partner has led a short suit, trying to find your length,
there is no hope. The diamonds are coming in without trouble and
your play is unlikely to matter. Against that, with only one point in
your hand, the chances are that partner has looked to his own length
and struck gold — provided you do not block up the mine! With declarer marked with a doubleton, partner has obviously led his lowest card and, irrespective of dummy's play, you must keep your ♣J
as an entry. An encouraging ♣7 is best.

North
♠ K 10 9
♥ 8 7 6
♦ K J 10 5 4
♣ 10 6

West
♠ 7 5 4
♥ J 5 3 2
♦ A 7
♣ A Q 9 8

East
♠ 8 3 2
♥ 10 9
♦ 6 3 2
♣ J 7 5 3 2

South
♠ A Q J 6
♥ A K Q 4
♦ Q 9 8
♣ K 4

At the table, declarer played well to call for the ♣10 and East duly
took the bait by going up; the defenders could now only take four
tricks when West regained the lead with the ♦A. Note that, in the
unlikely event of partner's having led from ♣K Q 9 8 (from which he
should probably prefer the lead of the ♣K), you will have only
given up an overtrick by playing low on the ♣10 (a point of concern
at pairs scoring only) since the clubs are irretrievably blocked; the ♣J
merely ensures a maximum of three club tricks for the defence.

Points to remember

1. With very weak hands, look out for every possibility of an entry, being re-
    luctant to part with potential entry cards prematurely.
2. Note the opening lead. West was reluctant to lead away from such a
    holding when well placed over a 2NT opener. Against that, with the
    bulk of the defensive strength in his hand, he realised that his partner was
    unlikely to get in and, therefore, that this was no time to stand on cer-
    emony.

Choose your moment!

Still on that theme, many players would go wrong in the following
type of situation:

Dealer West   **North**
N-S vulnerable   ♠ A Q 9 5

W	N	E	S
1NT¹	pass	pass	2♥
pass	3NT	pass	4♥

♥ 7 2

♦ Q J 10 4

¹ 12-14 points   ♣ K J 8

                                                               East

                                                               ♠ 6 3 2

                                                               ♥ 9 6

                                                               ♦ 6 3 2

                                                               ♣ A 7 5 4 2

West leads the ♣9 and dummy plays low. Which card do you play,
and would it make any difference if declarer called for the ♣K?

Your first duty is to consider the club position. The ♣9 surely denies a higher card; there is no holding including honours from which a nine would be led. So the ♣Q is with South (and he must also have the ♣10) so you must plan your defence on that assumption. On the bidding, the lead cannot be a singleton. You must hope that it is a doubleton and that West has an early trump trick. You can then give partner a third-round club ruff provided you keep your ♣A intact as entry. Regardless of dummy's card, you should encourage with the ♣7.

North
♠ A Q 9 5
♥ 7 2
♦ Q J 10 4
♣ K J 8

West
♠ K J 10 7
♥ A 5 3
♦ A 9 7 5
♣ 9 6

East
♠ 6 3 2
♥ 9 6
♦ 6 3 2
♣ A 7 5 4 2

South
♠ 8 4
♥ K Q J 10 8 4
♦ K 8
♣ Q 10 3

At the table, declarer, well aware of the threat, called for the ♣K and East duly dived into the well. After all, aces are there to catch kings, aren't they?

Points to remember

1. Note the importance of placing the outstanding club honours and realising that, in the context of the club suit itself, it is of little consequence when you take your ace. In the context of the whole hand, however, the timing is crucial.

2. Note also the good play by declarer, putting himself in opponents' shoes and trying to throw them off track.

3. These positions, of course, become less clear when the bidding does not rule out partner's lead being a singleton and you are left wondering whether you should rise, assuming the singleton, or duck, hoping for a doubleton with an early trump entry. There are no hard and fast rules and you have try to assess declarer's distribution and trump strength, according to his bidding, in order to decide which is the better bet.

Further situations in which the third-hand-high rule must be ignored arise when East is trying to establish his long suit against a no-trump contract and has few, if any entries outside that suit. In our companion book, *Focus on Declarer Play*, under the heading 'Lose the battle, win the war!', we pointed out that it is often in the best interests of both sides to lose the first round of a suit. This applies when declarer has one stopper and you have no entries outside your suit or when declarer has two stoppers and you have one entry outside with partner having led from a doubleton. Here it is important for partner to get in first to knock out the second stopper so that he can lead your long suit while your entry remains intact.

Let's look at some everyday positions. In the first group, East has overcalled with his long suit but has no quick entries outside:

a)
```
                     8 6 5
     7 2                            A K 10 9 3
                     Q J 4
```

b)
```
                     8 5 4 3
     7 2                            A Q J 10 9
                     K 6
```

c)
```
                     K 4
     10 7                           A Q 8 6 5 2
                     J 9 3
```

d)
```
                     K 4
     J 7                            A Q 8 6 5 2
                     10 9 3
```

e)
```
                     10 7 4
     9 5                            A J 8 6 5 2
                     K Q
```

f)
```
                     Q 6
     8 4                            A K J 9 3
                     10 7 5 2
```

In all these cases, East must refuse to win the first trick or lose the chance to bring in his suit.

In the next two examples, again the leader has a doubleton but East has one entry outside his suit and West is likely to get in early. This will typically arise when declarer's long suit looks something like this:

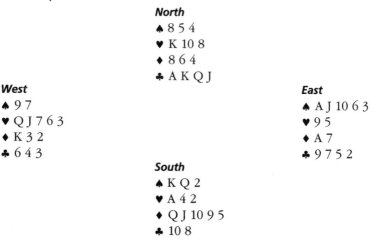

                          8 6 4
        K 3 2   A 7
                          Q J 10 9 5

On this next hand, West must be alert to the situation in order to act decisively at the critical moment.

North
♠ 8 5 4
♥ K 10 8
♦ 8 6 4
♣ A K Q J

West
♠ 9 7
♥ Q J 7 6 3
♦ K 3 2
♣ 6 4 3

East
♠ A J 10 6 3
♥ 9 5
♦ A 7
♣ 9 7 5 2

South
♠ K Q 2
♥ A 4 2
♦ Q J 10 9 5
♣ 10 8

North opens 1♣, East overcalls in spades, and South ends the auction by bidding game in no-trumps. West leads the ♠9, ducked to South.

Unfortunately for declarer, he has only eight tricks without a contribution from the diamond suit, and he is going to have to let the defenders in twice before he can get this suit going. It is vital that, West win the first round when declarer attacks diamonds, keeping East's ace intact. West now plays a second spade, and East clears the spade suit. Eventually, East will get in with the ♦K and cash two more spades to defeat the contract.

If, however, West carelessly ducks the first diamond, and East has to win it, it will do the defenders no good to set up their spade winners. When West wins the second diamond, he has no more spades, and his partner no longer has a high card through which his

spade winners can be reached.
      Similarly if we turn the hand round:

North
♠ K Q 2
♥ A J 5
♦ 8 6 4
♣ J 8 5 2

West
♠ A J 10 9 7
♥ 9 4
♦ A 7
♣ 9 6 4 3

East
♠ 5 3
♥ Q 10 8 7 6 3
♦ K 3 2
♣ 10 7

South
♠ 8 6 4
♥ K 2
♦ Q J 10 9 5
♣ A K Q

This time the play is harder to see since East needs to play high in second position in front of the concealed hand. Again South plays 3NT, but now West, the spade bidder, is on lead. The lead is the ♠J, won by the ♠Q, diamonds are started from dummy and East must rise with the ♦K to protect his partner's entry.

g)   Q 8 4
          7 2   K J 9 5 3
                       A 10 6

Here, if dummy plays low on West's 7, East must play low, or declarer will refuse the jack, killing the suit for good. If dummy plays the queen, East again must play low; otherwise declarer ducks with similar effect.

h)   8 4
          7 2   K Q J 9 5
                       A 10 6 3

If East plays an honour on trick one, declarer ducks and will concede only two tricks in the suit. If East ducks, the defenders will win three.

i)   A J 7 3
            5 4   K Q 10 6 2
                                9 8

Assuming declarer plays low on trick one, East must withhold his ten
to force South to win. Otherwise defenders take two tricks rather
than three.

j)   K 9
            6 4   A J 8 5 3 2
                                Q 10 7

If dummy plays the king, East must play low or lose the whole suit.

k)   8 5
            6 4   A Q J 9 2
                                K 10 7 3

East must play the nine on trick one. If he plays the jack or queen
instead, it will be allowed to hold and the defenders will be restricted to two tricks in the suit.

l)   8 5
            6 4   A K 10 3 2
                                Q J 9 7

Again, East must play low at trick one or be restricted to two tricks.

There are, of course, countless other suit combinations but these
should suffice to illustrate the point.

Let your honour interpose!

Another situation, where it is ill-advised to play third-hand high, arises when you will simply help declarer's communications:

				North
Dealer South				♠ 9 6 2
N-S vulnerable				♥ K J 9 8

W	N	E	S
			2♣
pass	2♦	pass	3NT[1]

North
♠ 9 6 2
♥ K J 9 8
♦ 8 7 5
♣ 8 6 3

[1] 25-27 points

East
♠ Q 10 7
♥ 10 7 5 3
♦ J 6
♣ J 10 9 5

Partner leads the ♥4 to dummy's ♥8. Which card do you play?

North
♠ 9 6 2
♥ K J 9 8
♦ 8 7 5
♣ 8 6 3

West
♠ K 8 4 3
♥ 6 4 2
♦ Q 10 4 2
♣ Q 7

East
♠ Q 10 7
♥ 10 7 5 3
♦ J 6
♣ J 10 9 5

South
♠ A J 5
♥ A Q
♦ A K 9 3
♣ A K 4 2

Regardless of the position of the ♥Q, it cannot gain to put in the ♥10. Declarer can always take a finesse on the second round if he needs it. Playing high is fatal in this position, as South is now able to take four heart tricks instead of three — the difference between success and failure as there are only five top tricks outside the suit. As it happens, it would have been safe for West to lead either of his long suits but, sitting over a huge hand, either of these leads could have been the only one to give away the contract.

Points to remember

1. Consider the likely positions in the suit led before playing mechanically.
2. Note the choice of lead. In this kind of position, where there is a massive hand facing a likely near Yarborough, passive defence is very often right. Admittedly, a heart lead might pick up partner's honour holding (so you might be asking for trouble) but South could be solid. Lead a non-heart suit and you are definitely courting danger.

2

The Silver Lining

We now turn to timing as it relates to trump contracts. Charging in with trumps at the wrong moment is one of the biggest sources of major losses on defence for many players. Remember that trumps are a powerful weapon, but like many powerful weapons can be injurious to the user if not handled properly.

Ruff with suspicion in second position!

Here is a very simple example in which declarer was presented with a hopeless slam:

Dealer South
E-W vulnerable

W	N	E	S
			2NT[1]
pass	3♣[2]	pass	3♥
pass	5♥	pass	6♥

[1] 20-22 points
[2] Stayman

North
♠ A 6
♥ Q 8 6 2
♦ J 7 6 4 3 2
♣ A

East
♠ Q 7 3 2
♥ 10 9 5 4
♦ —
♣ J 8 6 4 3

You resist the temptation to double for a diamond lead and partner leads the ♠J to dummy's ♠A, declarer playing the ♠4. Somewhat to your surprise, declarer now calls for a low diamond. How do you defend?

Simply asking yourself what the positions are in the red suits will save you from going wrong here. What is South's diamond holding and why isn't he drawing trumps? If you decline to take a decision until you have answered these questions, you will reach the conclusion that it can hardly be right to ruff. If South is intending to take a finesse, say with ♦ A Q doubleton, you will simply be ruffing partner's trick. Furthermore, while the bidding has placed the two top hearts with South, there is no law against partner's holding a singleton jack in which case you have a natural trump trick. By ruffing, you are simply coalescing your two tricks into one to save declarer.

Alternatively, South could have ♦A K doubleton and be trying to arrange ruffs. But that would leave partner with queen to five diamonds and declarer with a lot of ruffing to do. Eventually, if you hold on to your trumps, one of them is bound to be promoted — refusal to ruff is most unlikely to cost.

North
♠ A 6
♥ Q 8 6 2
♦ J 7 6 4 3 2
♣ A

West
♠ J 10 9 5
♥ J
♦ Q 9 8
♣ Q 10 7 5 2

East
♠ Q 7 3 2
♥ 10 9 5 4
♦ —
♣ J 8 6 4 3

South
♠ K 8 4
♥ A K 7 3
♦ A K 10 5
♣ K 9

Points to remember

1. Think twice before ruffing in second position, particularly when you are likely to be ruffing declarer's loser. At best, you will break even; often it will cost.

2. Note declarer's play: realising that the slam was only in danger if both red suits broke badly, he put East to the test as early as possible. One round of trumps would have given the show away: East has little temptation to ruff with his certain trump trick. As it is, a round of diamonds is most unlikely to cost. If East shows out, a trick must be lost in the suit anyway. If West ruffs, there is a marked finesse in diamonds and the ruff will almost certainly be made by the hand with long trumps.

Don't ruff partner's trick!

The number of players who do ruff in the kind of position we have
just seen, weakening their own trump holding and effectively ruffing their partner's trick, is alarming. Even with a hopeless trump
holding like two small, ruffing is usually wrong. Having seen the
previous hand, can you explain why it may be fatal to ruff here?

North
- ♠ A
- ♥ A J 9 6
- ♦ K J 7 6 3 2
- ♣ K 8

West
- ♠ J 9 5 3 2
- ♥ Q 10 8 5 4
- ♦ 9
- ♣ J 6

Dealer South
N-S vulnerable

W	N	E	S
			1NT[1]
pass	2♣[2]	pass	2♥
pass	3♠[3]	pass	4♣
pass	5♣	pass	5♦
pass	5NT[4]	pass	6♦[5]
pass	6♥		

[1] 15-17 points
[2] Stayman
[3] agrees hearts, no spade
  losers
[4] grand slam force
[5] one of top three honours

You lead your diamond to the ♦J, ♦Q and ♦A. South plays the
♥K, partner discarding the ♣2. He continues with the ♦8; how do
you defend?

You can see that, if you ruff, you leave yourself with three trumps which can be picked up with the aid of two finesses. After that, the diamond suit plus whatever black tops North-South hold will fulfil the contract.

It cannot therefore cost to decline to ruff, keeping your trump trick intact. Furthermore, discarding a black card allows your partner to score a diamond trick to defeat the contract.

```
                        North
                        ♠ A
                        ♥ A J 9 6
                        ♦ K J 7 6 3 2
                        ♣ K 8
West                                            East
♠ J 9 5 3 2                                     ♠ Q 10 8 6 4
♥ Q 10 8 5 4                                    ♥ —
♦ 9                                             ♦ Q 10 4
♣ J 6                                           ♣ 10 9 4 3 2
                        South
                        ♠ K 7
                        ♥ K 7 3 2
                        ♦ A 8 5
                        ♣ A Q 7 5
```

Points to remember

1. Where you have a certain trump trick by sheer weight of numbers, it cannot run away; it therefore costs nothing to discard instead of ruffing.

2. Despite the trump stack, it is wise not to double these contracts and especially here where the opponents were thinking about a grand slam and may well be able to stand the bad split. Doubling warns declarer of impending trouble before it is too late and, in any case, consideration of the odds rules it out completely. Assuming the contract goes one off, your gain is 100. If it is made, the loss is 230 (if they don't redouble). Already it is more than 2:1 against. More serious is that if, as a result of the double, the contract is made when it would have been beaten, the loss is 1760. A further point is that the opponents may remove to 6NT, easily made by conceding a diamond. Now the loss is 1540. For the double to be right, you should be very confident of three things:

    a) the contract is going at least two off,

    b) doubling will not help declarer to save a trick,

    c) there is no escape to a better contract; if they run, you can confidently double again.

Don't give partner away!

In this next example, your trumps are weaker.

Dealer West				**North**
E-W vulnerable				♠ K 10 6

W	*N*	*E*	*S*
2♠[1]	2NT	pass	3♣[2]
pass	3♦	pass	3♥
pass	4♣[3]	pass	4NT
pass	5♦	pass	6♥

North
♠ K 10 6
♥ 10 8 6 2
♦ A K Q J 9
♣ K

East
♠ 4 2
♥ 9 5 4
♦ 7 4 3
♣ 10 9 8 4 3

[1] weak
[2] Baron, asking for 4-card
 suits up the line
[3] cue bid agreeing hearts

Partner leads the ♠Q and declarer can hardly wait to win it in hand, take a finesse of the ♠10 at trick two and then play the ♠K. How do you defend?

All you need to do is ask yourself why declarer has played like this. Is there a desperate rush to discard a loser? If so, what loser? What cannot be discarded on diamonds later? Has South got a singleton club, despite his no-trump bid? That would leave partner with six to go with his six spades. In that case, declarer would just draw trumps and discard the club loser later. Why hasn't declarer drawn trumps? That is the crucial question! The answer is, of course, that he does not know how to do so and will remain ignorant unless you tell him!

North
♠ K 10 6
♥ 10 8 6 2
♦ A K Q J 9
♣ K

West
♠ Q J 9 8 7 5
♥ Q 7
♦ 8 6
♣ A 5 2

East
♠ 4 2
♥ 9 5 4
♦ 7 4 3
♣ 10 9 8 4 3

South
♠ A 3
♥ A K J 3
♦ 10 5 2
♣ Q J 7 6

You now realise what is going on. If you ruff, he will assume that you have no honour to protect and will probably play for the drop in hearts. If you refuse, however, he is likely to credit you with a trump holding worth keeping and take the percentage line of the finesse. The number of people who ruff in this position is even greater than that in the previous example.

Points to remember

1.   Insist on finding a satisfactory explanation of declarer's line of play before choosing your plan of defence.
2.   In this kind of position, where declarer does not draw trumps, it is likely that partner has a holding of interest; help him by keeping enemy blinds down!

Don't win tricks twice over!

We have looked at two situations in which the hand with the shortage must refrain from ruffing, irrespective of the quality of his trumps. Equally, the partner of the hand with shortness must be wary of giving a ruff when declarer is the only likely beneficiary. Again, an embarrassingly large number of defenders would go wrong here:

Dealer East
N-S vulnerable

W	N	E	S
		pass	1♦
2♠[1]	3♣	3♠	4♦
pass	5♦		

[1] weak

North
♠ A 9
♥ 10 3 2
♦ A 10 9
♣ K Q 10 9 5

East
♠ Q 10 7 4
♥ 9 6 4
♦ 7 5
♣ A J 7 6

According to the Law of Total Tricks you might well have decided to bid 4♠ rather than 3♠, but that is a discussion for a different book. Partner leads the ♣2, which can only be a singleton. Dummy's ♣K is played. How do you defend?

South clearly has a singleton spade and you will get nowhere in that suit. It is perfectly in order to duck the club at trick one as your two club tricks can hardly run away. But, if you win, you must switch to a heart as the only hope of defeating the contract.

Consider the consequences of giving partner a club ruff. That could well be the end of the defence. West may not be able to attack hearts effectively from his side and, even if he can, it might be too late. South wins, draws two rounds of trumps, plays the ♣Q, discarding a heart, and ruffs out your ♣J. Returning to dummy via the ♦A or ♠A, he enjoys the remaining clubs, discarding his last heart. Three clubs, six trumps and two major aces total eleven.

North
♠ A 9
♥ 10 3 2
♦ A 10 9
♣ K Q 10 9 5

West
♠ K J 8 5 3 2
♥ K J 7 5
♦ 6 3
♣ 2

East
♠ Q 10 7 4
♥ 9 6 4
♦ 7 5
♣ A J 7 6

South
♠ 6
♥ A Q 8
♦ K Q J 8 4 2
♣ 8 4 3

Points to remember

1. Beware of playing on declarer's long suit unless it is clear that this is the only way to defeat the contract. The chances are that you will be helping his, rather than your, cause and that, at best, you will break even. But you should not criticise partner for leading his club. If you had held :

    ♠ A x x x ♥ x x x ♦ x x ♣ A x x x.

    and he had started with a spade, would you have found the switch to the ♣A? A club is also probably the only lead to defeat the contract if you have a similar hand including the ♦A instead of the ♣A, unless again you are clairvoyant enough to find the club switch after winning your ♠A at trick one.

2. Notice the importance of assessing the count in the spade suit so that you make the correct major-suit switch.

Avoid the overkill!

So far, we have discussed hands where it is wrong to ruff in second position under an honour. The same applies when you are in third position and partner has led the suit. Be particularly wary of ruffing when it is clear that you are merely ruffing partner's trick.

Dealer West
Neither vulnerable

W	N	E	S
2♥[1]	pass	3♥	3♠
pass	4♠		

[1] weak

North
♠ J 9
♥ 10 4 3
♦ K Q 9 5
♣ K 7 5 4

West
♠ 3 2
♥ K Q J 7 5 2
♦ 10 8 6 2
♣ 2

You lead the ♣2 to the ♣4, ♣9 and South's ♣A. The ♠5 runs to the ♠3, ♠9 and partner's ♠A. Partner returns the ♣Q to declarer's ♣3. How do you defend?

You should realise that there is nothing to be gained by ruffing and, more important, that if you do, you allow the ♣K to remain intact; that could be a crucial entry to the diamond honours. This is critical when partner has the ♦A:

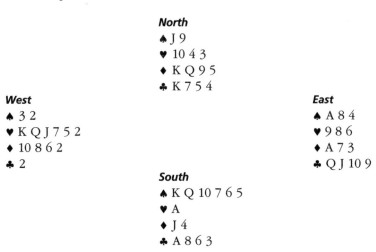

North
♠ J 9
♥ 10 4 3
♦ K Q 9 5
♣ K 7 5 4

West
♠ 3 2
♥ K Q J 7 5 2
♦ 10 8 6 2
♣ 2

East
♠ A 8 4
♥ 9 8 6
♦ A 7 3
♣ Q J 10 9

South
♠ K Q 10 7 6 5
♥ A
♦ J 4
♣ A 8 6 3

Try playing it both ways. If you ruff, nothing can prevent declarer from drawing trumps, conceding the ♦A and making the contract with five spade tricks, the ♥A, two diamonds and two clubs. Now try discarding instead of ruffing: the ♣K has to win and declarer is doomed. If he draws trumps and concedes the ♦A (as he must to have any chance), he loses two clubs and the two aces for one down.

Points to remember
1. Note that declarer won the first club in hand, firstly to ensure that his remaining honour sat over the hand likely to be ruffing and secondly to maintain an entry to the diamonds.
2. Before ruffing, consider the likely situation in the suit and whether you are ruffing winners or losers. It could be right to ruff if you still have two trumps and can organise a further ruff. Partner should indicate which red ace he has with the size of the club he returns. If East held the ♥A, it would be correct for him to play the ♣Q at trick one and return the ♣J later.

2

Communications Issues

So far we have looked at a number of situations where it is right for defenders to restrain themselves, since taking action will help declarer more than themselves. In his famous book, *Why you lose at bridge*, S. J. Simon criticised defenders for 'getting busy at the wrong moment', i.e. attempting risky defences when passive defence is in order. Nevertheless, just as common is the converse — failure to attack when it is crucial to do so. It is in the attacking process that some of the defenders' worst problems can occur — the problems implicit in keeping lines of communication open.

A blocked drain is defenders' pain!

It is vital to ensure that the defenders' suit does not get blocked; it might be worthwhile sacrificing a high card 'unnecessarily' to achieve this. The following situation is commonly misdefended:

Dealer West
N-S vulnerable

W	N	E	S
pass	1♦	pass	1NT
pass	2NT	pass	3NT

North
♠ A K 8
♥ K J 8
♦ K 8 3 2
♣ A 7 6

East
♠ J 9 6 5
♥ Q 10 6 4
♦ A 5
♣ 4 3 2

Partner leads the ♦Q and dummy plays low. How do you defend?

It seems automatic for you to play low as well, hoping that declarer will misguess on the next round; after all, the lead could have been from ♦ A Q J 10 x. But there is no need for declarer to commit himself at trick two; he can play low again, and the suit is hopelessly blocked. West would need two side-suit entries, one to knock out the ♦K, the other to cash his winners, and that clearly is not on. South may be credited with about eight points; you have seven and there are eighteen in dummy. That leaves seven for partner, including the ♦ Q J. Four points remain — one trick perhaps, but certainly not two.

North
♠ A K 8
♥ K J 8
♦ K 8 3 2
♣ A 7 6

West
♠ 7 4 2
♥ 7 5 3
♦ Q J 10 9 7
♣ K J

East
♠ J 9 6 5
♥ Q 10 6 4
♦ A 5
♣ 4 3 2

South
♠ Q 10 3
♥ A 9 2
♦ 6 4
♣ Q 10 9 8 5

You must therefore rise with the ♦A and continue the suit, so that the ♦K is removed from dummy while partner's presumed entry remains intact.

Points to remember

1. Doubleton honours are dangerous toys; very often, it is right to play the honour first.
2. Note the way it was confirmed that partner cannot have two entries outside diamonds. Get into the habit of working out at least the approximate point-count of the unseen hands; it will often save you from making unrealistic assumptions. This particularly applies in no-trump contracts when you can usually count points fairly accurately. In suit contracts, players may have bid up on distributional hands and now it is more difficult. However, there is still no excuse for not making the effort. If you still go wrong then, at least, you will have tried!

Kings are there to catch queens — but it works both ways!

It is worthwhile to do some practice on these positions because they occur so frequently. Here is another example.

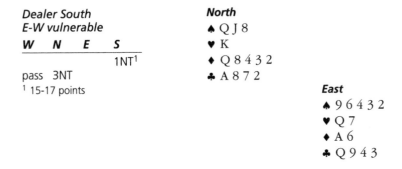

Dealer South
E-W vulnerable

W	N	E	S
			1NT[1]
pass	3NT		

[1] 15-17 points

North
♠ Q J 8
♥ K
♦ Q 8 4 3 2
♣ A 8 7 2

East
♠ 9 6 4 3 2
♥ Q 7
♦ A 6
♣ Q 9 4 3

Partner leads the ♥J to dummy's ♥K, South following with the ♥2. Declarer now calls for a low diamond. How do you defend?

Once again, a roll-call on points will keep you on the right track. There are twelve in dummy and you have eight, totalling twenty to leave twenty. Even giving South a minimum, partner can have no more than five and that includes the ♥J. He can therefore only have one trick outside and you must keep his entry intact by rising with the ♦A and returning your remaining heart — the ♥7, of course!

North
- ♠ Q J 8
- ♥ K
- ♦ Q 8 4 3 2
- ♣ A 8 7 2

West
- ♠ 7 5
- ♥ J 10 9 8 6 4
- ♦ K 9
- ♣ J 10 5

East
- ♠ 9 6 4 3 2
- ♥ Q 7
- ♦ A 6
- ♣ Q 9 4 3

South
- ♠ A K 10
- ♥ A 5 3 2
- ♦ J 10 7 5
- ♣ K 6

You did play the ♥Q at trick one, didn't you? If you did not, South will refuse the second round of hearts, leaving you on play and with no hope of establishing the suit before the diamonds come in.

Points to remember

1. Don't take full credit for playing the ♥Q at trick one unless you also realised that, not only were you covering the position above but also that in which South has the ♦K and the hearts are:

K

A J 10 8 x x   Q 7

9 x x x

Here again, if you kept the ♥Q, partner cannot overtake without promoting the ♥9 to a second stopper.

2. There are many more positions where an unblock is necessary, e.g.

A

Q J 10 8 6 5   K 4

9 7 3 2

The queen is led — the king must be played now.

The best way to be selfish is to be unselfish!

So far, we have considered positions in no-trump contracts and, in practice, these form the vast majority of hands where unblocking plays are needed. But beware! Suit contracts are by no means exempt:

Dealer North
N-S vulnerable

W	N	E	S
	1♦	pass	1♥
1♠	3♥	pass	4♥

North
♠ A 8 4
♥ K Q 8 4
♦ A J 6 5
♣ A 8

East
♠ K 2
♥ 9 6
♦ K 3 2
♣ 9 7 5 4 3 2

Partner leads the ♠Q to dummy's ♠A. How do you defend?

Again — at the risk of getting boring — a points roll-call will keep you out of a very unpleasant post-mortem. There are eighteen points in dummy and six in your hand to total twenty-four and partner has already indicated the ♠ Q J. Even giving South a minimum six points (he may well have more), the total is thirty-three, leaving seven unaccounted for. Partner could have two tricks but may well only have one. A likely scenario is this:

North
♠ A 8 4
♥ K Q 8 4
♦ A J 6 5
♣ A 8

West
♠ Q J 10 9 6
♥ A 5
♦ 9 8 4
♣ Q J 10

East
♠ K 2
♥ 9 6
♦ K 3 2
♣ 9 7 5 4 3 2

South
♠ 7 5 3
♥ J 10 7 3 2
♦ Q 10 7
♣ K 6

Observe the effect of playing your low spade at trick one. Declarer attacks trumps, West winning. You will win the next spade and exit in trumps or clubs, leaving South time to knock out your ♦K while West is unable to cash a second spade trick. Later, dummy's long diamond will be cashed for declarer's tenth trick while he discards his losing spade. Play your ♠K at trick one, however, and the drain is clear for the defence to take two spade tricks immediately plus the ♥A and ♦K to total four tricks — one down.

Points to remember

1. Even if partner has overcalled on a very poor suit, all need not be lost if partner has the ♥A; you are able to ruff the third round of spades.

2. Even if partner does not have the trump ace, you are still saved by the unblock if his spades are as good as Q J 9 x x. You will now be able to lead through South's ten.

3. Doubleton honour holdings are loaded with dynamite and, if you pick them up and are defending, at least consider whether it might be wise to play the honour on the first round.

Trumps in dummy could serve two purposes!

We now turn to strategies for disrupting declarer's pleasure. When it is obvious that he has the tricks necessary for his contract, look for ways to spoil his fun.

When declarer has a long suit in dummy, attack the entries. This can be accomplished in three ways:

a) Play the suit itself prematurely so that declarer runs out before trumps are drawn. This is likely to be applicable when dummy has no obvious side-suit entries.

b) Attack side-suit top cards so that they are removed prematurely. This is likely when the side-suit needs to be ruffed high and declarer will therefore obviously not be able to play the suit from hand.

c) Force dummy to ruff so that dummy's trumps are shortened and declarer cannot complete the drawing of trumps in dummy after the long suit has been ruffed high.

Dealer North
Neither vulnerable

W	N	E	S
	1♦	pass	1♥
dbl	3♦	pass	4♥

North
♠ Q J 8
♥ A K 4
♦ K J 9 8 7 2
♣ Q

West
♠ A K 10 7 6
♥ 9 8
♦ 6 5
♣ A 9 7 3

North's 3♦ bid implies some interest in hearts, since with a strong hand which is very short of hearts, he would redouble, indicating in interest in defence. He can always repeat his diamonds later, if appropriate.

You cash the two top spades, partner following with the ♠2 and ♠3 while South plays the ♠4 and ♠5. How do you continue? Would it make any difference if you held the ♣K rather than the ♣A?

Partner has indicated a trebleton spade and you should notice that he had a choice of cards to play on the second round of the suit. In such situations, you should get into the habit of taking the opportunity to indicate suit preference. Trumps and spades are out of consideration and thus a high spade at trick two would suggest the higher-ranking of the remaining suits, diamonds, while here the low card expresses interest in clubs. This knowledge gives you the opportunity to attack dummy's trump entries to the diamonds. Cash the ♣A, hoping that partner encourages, and then play a low club, forcing dummy to ruff. The long diamonds are now dead and, although declarer is able to ruff two clubs in dummy, the lack of entries to hand results in his losing a trump trick.

<pre>
                        North
                        ♠ Q J 8
                        ♥ A K 4
                        ♦ K J 9 8 7 2
                        ♣ Q
West   East
♠ A K 10 7 6   ♠ 9 3 2
♥ 9 8   ♥ 10 5 2
♦ 6 5   ♦ Q 10 3
♣ A 9 7 3   ♣ K 8 6 5
                        South
                        ♠ 5 4
                        ♥ Q J 7 6 3
                        ♦ A 4
                        ♣ J 10 4 2
</pre>

If you hold the ♣K instead of the ♣A, you must still play that. Again, playing a low club sets you up for a ruffing finesse on the second round.

Points to remember

1. Note the opportunity to signal in situations where a defender has a trebleton in his partner's suit and has shown count (with the lowest card) on the first round.
2. Note the club position and the necessity for the defender sitting under the shortage to play his high card and then lead low through the shortage.

Make declarer eat his dessert first!

Having seen the idea, see if you can recognise the approach required in this next example.

Dealer West
N-S vulnerable

W	N	E	S
1♣	1♦	2♠[1]	3♥
pass	4♥		

[1] pre-emptive

North
♠ 10 6 5
♥ Q
♦ A K Q J 7 2
♣ 8 5 3

West
♠ A K 3
♥ K 6 4 2
♦ 10 3
♣ Q J 9 6

You lead the ♠A, partner following with the ♠Q and South the ♠8. How do you continue?

South will surely not follow to a second spade but, even if he can, you have only three obvious tricks in the majors. Your first priority is to worry about those diamonds. South's plan will be to draw trumps and enjoy that side suit and your only hope is to strip him of it prematurely. You must switch to diamonds at once and partner's duty will be to give count (here encouragement/discouragement is obviously irrelevant as the defenders are not going to get rich on diamonds!) Assuming he shows a trebleton, when you get in with the ♥K, you will play a second diamond to cut dummy and declarer adrift before trumps have been drawn. You can then sit back and wait for your club trick(s).

If South started with three diamonds, you never had a chance anyway. If he has only one, he will have to cash his second top card immediately after your diamond switch (or go without it) and the position will then be clear to you.

North
♠ 10 6 5
♥ Q
♦ A K Q J 7 2
♣ 8 5 3

West
♠ A K 3
♥ K 6 4 2
♦ 10 3
♣ Q J 9 6

East
♠ Q J 9 7 4 2
♥ 5 3
♦ 8 5 4
♣ 7 4

South
♠ 8
♥ A J 10 9 8 7
♦ 9 6
♣ A K 10 2

Points to remember

1. Note the necessity for East to give his partner the relevant information on diamonds — the count.

2. If dummy has plenty of side entries and diamonds are played, signalling suit preference is likely to take first priority.

Attack the side door!

Sometimes, it is necessary to attack side-suit entries to stop declarer cashing high cards:

					North
Dealer West					♠ A J
Neither vulnerable					♥ A K 7 4 2
W	**N**	**E**	**S**		♦ K 10 5
1♥	1NT	2♦	4♠		♣ 10 9 3

West
♠ 6 3
♥ Q J 10 9 5 3
♦ A J
♣ A 7 6

You lead the ♥Q, won in dummy, East following with the ♥6 and South the ♥8. South plays the ♠A, to which he follows with the ♠4 from hand, and cashes the ♠J, partner echoing with the ♠5 and ♠2 and South following to the second round with the ♠8. The ♣10 runs to East's ♣4, South's ♣5, and your ♣A. How do you defend?

With East having indicated a third trump, you can see South's problem. He fears trying to cash the second top heart, which may be ruffed. So why did he not draw all the trumps and lead towards the ♦K for an entry? If you can answer that, you can see the solution. If he plays this way, he will ensure his second heart trick but will only be able to play clubs once from dummy when he actually needs to play them twice:

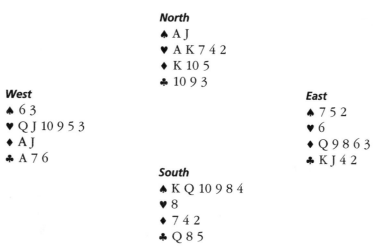

North
♠ A J
♥ A K 7 4 2
♦ K 10 5
♣ 10 9 3

West
♠ 6 3
♥ Q J 10 9 5 3
♦ A J
♣ A 7 6

East
♠ 7 5 2
♥ 6
♦ Q 9 8 6 3
♣ K J 4 2

South
♠ K Q 10 9 8 4
♥ 8
♦ 7 4 2
♣ Q 8 5

This way, however, he hopes that you will persist with hearts, which he will ruff in hand. He will then draw the remaining trump and lead a diamond, later discarding his third diamond on the top heart and leading another club towards the ♣Q. To disrupt this, you must take your ♣A and play ace and another diamond at once, removing dummy's entry prematurely. The top heart is now stranded and, although South can play his second round of clubs, partner will win, and cash the ♦Q for the defenders' fourth trick.

Points to remember

1. Notice partner's echo in trumps to indicate a holding of three and/or a desire to ruff. Unlike you, he does not know that South is also out of hearts.

2. If declarer refuses to draw trumps in situations where it appears to be easy to do so, insist on knowing why. The reason will often be a guide to the whereabouts of the outstanding high cards.

Kings are there to catch queens . . but some ladies are best avoided!

In situations where the stronger enemy hand finishes as dummy, you must visualise the hidden threat and spoil the entries to hand.

Dealer North
Both vulnerable

W	N	E	S
	1♦	pass	1NT
pass	3NT		

North
♠ Q 7 5
♥ K 8 3 2
♦ A Q J 10
♣ A Q

East
♠ J 10 6 4
♥ 5
♦ K 6 4 2
♣ K 6 5 3

Partner leads the ♥Q and the ♥K wins in dummy. On the ♣A, you play the ♣5, declarer the ♣2 and partner the ♣4. Now follows the ♣Q. How do you defend?

There are a number of points about this hand. Firstly, the bidding indicates that South, if anything, is interested in clubs. Secondly, note that you are not in a position to return an early heart. Thirdly, South has limited his hand in terms of point count and is likely to have only one side-suit entry. If you take your ♣K now, you may well allow South several club tricks as here:

North
♠ Q 7 5
♥ K 8 3 2
♦ A Q J 10
♣ A Q

West		East
♠ A 3 2		♠ J 10 6 4
♥ Q J 10 9 6		♥ 5
♦ 9 8		♦ K 6 4 2
♣ 9 8 4		♣ K 6 5 3

South
♠ K 9 8
♥ A 7 4
♦ 7 5 3
♣ J 10 7 2

But that is not the full story. Take full credit only if you realised that, after you have ducked the club and declarer continues with the ♦A and a further diamond, you should win and return a diamond rather than risk opening up the spade suit. Declarer has eight tricks on top (one spade, two hearts, three diamonds and two clubs) and a spade from you will allow him a ninth. Also, if declarer calls for a spade from dummy, the chances are that he will rise with his ♠K, but you still should split your honours to ensure defeating the contract — this can never cost.

Points to remember

1. Observe that declarer won the first trick in dummy to preserve his precious entry to the weak hand.

2. Note that ducking the club restricts declarer to two club tricks instead of three.

3. In this kind of position, where declarer has communication problems and no obvious long suit, passive defence is usually right. In a race situation it could well be right to attack spades, but not here.

Information Theory

1

Throwing the Switch

In life we often have to summon up the courage to admit we were wrong; the same is true at the bridge table. In particular, there is no shame in discovering, after seeing dummy, that the opening lead does not in fact represent the defenders' best chance. This primarily applies to no-trump contracts: when it is clear that declarer has a suit well stopped, do not be afraid to try another.

Don't flog a dead horse!

We shall start with a simple example which was misdefended at many tables when it cropped up in a tournament.

Dealer North			
N-S vulnerable			
W	**N**	**E**	**S**
	1♣	1♠	3NT

North
♠ 8 7
♥ A 10 5
♦ 9 3
♣ A K J 10 5 2

East
♠ A J 10 9 6
♥ J 9 6
♦ K 7 5 2
♣ 9

Partner leads the ♠4 and dummy follows. How do you defend?

This is a just a question of being realistic. Does that ♠4 really come from three to an honour? South has confidently bid the no-trump game, without consulting his partner, and should surely have a double stopper. With the clubs almost certainly coming in for six tricks, you must beat the contract now or never. You are hardly going to get rich quick on hearts and must therefore win the first trick and turn to diamonds, starting with the usual fourth-highest ♦2.

North
♠ 8 7
♥ A 10 5
♦ 9 3
♣ A K J 10 5 2

West
♠ 4 3
♥ 8 7 4 3 2
♦ A Q 10 6
♣ 8 7

East
♠ A J 10 9 6
♥ J 9 6
♦ K 7 5 2
♣ 9

South
♠ K Q 5 2
♥ K Q
♦ J 8 4
♣ Q 6 4 3

Points to remember

1.   Where it is obvious that declarer, given the slightest chance, is going to run for home, do not hesitate to adopt desperate measures.

2.   Decide which switch is most likely to bring in the number of tricks required by the defenders and choose accordingly.

Know when you are beaten!

The previous tip applies with even greater force when dummy comes down with a pleasant surprise for declarer in the form of an honour in the 'danger' suit. In that case, you must hope that the opponents have an overkill position in that area and again look elsewhere. The following hand was misdefended in an international match:

Dealer East
N-S vulnerable

W	N	E	S
		1♥	1NT
pass	2NT	pass	3NT

North
♠ 10 6 2
♥ Q 6
♦ 6 4 3 2
♣ A Q 9 2

East
♠ A J 9 4
♥ A 10 9 8 7 5
♦ Q 7
♣ J

Partner dutifully leads the ♥3 and dummy plays low. How do you defend?

Here, with dummy having produced an extra heart honour, there is little hope in that suit. With twelve points in your hand and the opponents in game, partner can hardly be expected to produce more than three or four. If you are to defeat the contract in diamonds, he would need at least the ace and jack — five points, which is just not on. But there is a chance that he holds the ♠K, and your correct defence is to win the first heart and switch to the ♠J.

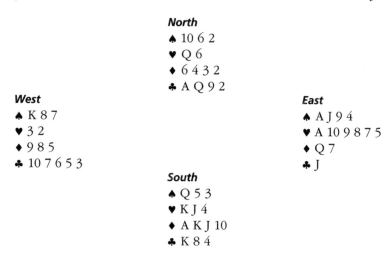

North
♠ 10 6 2
♥ Q 6
♦ 6 4 3 2
♣ A Q 9 2

West
♠ K 8 7
♥ 3 2
♦ 9 8 5
♣ 10 7 6 5 3

East
♠ A J 9 4
♥ A 10 9 8 7 5
♦ Q 7
♣ J

South
♠ Q 5 3
♥ K J 4
♦ A K J 10
♣ K 8 4

Declarer has no answer and must lose the first five tricks.

Points to remember

1. Just to ram the point home, it is just possible that partner had led from ♥ J 4 3, in which case there is justification in concentrating on hearts. But closer examination reveals that the logic does not stand up. You have credited partner with one point in the ♥J and cannot count on him for more than two others. Make that the ♠Q and, if you play on hearts, declarer may well be able to run home anyway with one heart trick and, with your honours dropping early, eight tricks in the minors. The spade switch offers a much better chance.

2. Notice that declarer played low in dummy, making a duck by you at trick one more attractive.

3. It is critical that the switch is to the ♠J, and no other card. More on this after the next hand.

Be suspicious of a hearty appetite!

Having seen the previous idea, try this next example which is perhaps less obvious:

Dealer East
N-S vulnerable

W	N	E	S
		1♥	1NT[1]
pass	3NT		

[1] 15-17 points

North
♠ 9 6 2
♥ A 7 2
♦ 6 4 3
♣ A K 5 2

East
♠ K 10 8 4
♥ K J 9 8 6 5
♦ A 8
♣ 9

Again, partner dutifully leads the ♥3 and dummy plays low. How do you defend this time?

Declarer must have the remaining hearts and therefore a double stopper. You will certainly get in once with the ♦A but the ♠K is unlikely to be useful. Playing on hearts, therefore, is simply flogging the dead horse. Give partner modest in help in spades, however, and you might be able to arrange three tricks in that suit to go with your two red winners. This time, the correct card to lead, after winning the first heart, is the ♠10 to cover this position:

North
♠ 9 6 2
♥ A 7 2
♦ 6 4 3
♣ A K 5 2

West
♠ Q 7 5
♥ 3
♦ 9 7 5 2
♣ J 10 7 6 3

East
♠ K 10 8 4
♥ K J 9 8 6 5
♦ A 8
♣ 9

South
♠ A J 3
♥ Q 10 4
♦ K Q J 10
♣ Q 8 4

Points to remember

1. Observe that declarer did not rise with the ♥A to avoid the immediate spade switch. He is likely to need two heart tricks for his contract so the best time to persuade you to go wrong is at trick one.

2. Note the choice of the middle spade card to trap declarer's ♠J and set up a tenace position over dummy's ♠9. The lead of the middle honour in these last two examples is known as a 'surround play'. The easiest way to illustrate the need to lead the specified card is to try the alternatives. On this hand, if you start with the ♠4, declarer will duck in hand, forcing West to win the ♠Q, and leaving South with the ♠AJ over East's ♠K.

    I leave it to the reader as an exercise to try the alternatives in the previous example and satisfy himself that, unless East starts with the ♠J, declarer will be able to make a trick in the suit, one to which he is not entitled.

Assassinate the right king!

An estimate of partner's likely point-count will often constitute a
guide as to whether the horse you are flogging is still alive:

Dealer East				**North**
N-S vulnerable				♠ J 10 4

W	**N**	**E**	**S**
		pass	1NT[1]
pass	3NT		

[1] 15-17 points

North
♠ J 10 4
♥ 6 5 3
♦ A K Q 8
♣ J 10 9

West
♠ A 9 5
♥ 10 9 8 2
♦ 10 6 4
♣ A Q 7

You lead the ♥10 to partner's ♥Q and declarer's ♥A. Declarer
crosses to the ♦A, partner playing the ♦2, and runs the ♣J to partner's ♣3 and his own ♣2. How do you defend?

Even giving South a minimum fifteen points, you can see that, with twenty-one more on view, partner can have started with four at most and he has already shown the ♥Q. The ♥K, therefore, can safely be credited to South and any hopes of success in that suit are ruled out. The only card which could help defeat the contract is the ♠Q and you should credit it to East. Now, if he has a five-card suit, South's ♠K will crash on the second round and you can cash three more tricks when in with the ♣A. You should therefore win this trick and switch to the ♠A and another spade.

<pre>
                        North
                        ♠ J 10 4
                        ♥ 6 5 3
                        ♦ A K Q 8
                        ♣ J 10 9
West   East
♠ A 9 5   ♠ Q 8 7 3 2
♥ 10 9 8 2   ♥ Q 4
♦ 10 6 4   ♦ 7 3 2
♣ A Q 7   ♣ 6 4 3
                        South
                        ♠ K 6
                        ♥ A K J 7
                        ♦ J 9 5
                        ♣ K 8 5 2
</pre>

A low spade, ducked by partner, is also good enough but why not make the position crystal clear, giving him as little chance as possible to go wrong?

Points to remember

1. Your line of defence must always be consistent with the bidding and play to date. Yes, you will always get opponents who open a point light (partner having the ♥K after all!) and look silly when you fail to continue the suit. My advice is that, if you regularly believe opponents, you will be right more often than not and it seems preferable to look silly playing correctly than playing for something against the weight of the evidence. In the long run, if not on a given hand, you will beat players who 'shade' and make anti-system bids but you will have to accept the occasional deception.

2. Getting into more advanced areas of defensive signalling, we might

have commented on East's first diamond. Many partnerships play 'Smith' echoes. This system of signalling demands that, in a situation where:

a)   it is not clear to West whether he should persist with the suit he led or switch, and

b)   the count and attitude towards diamonds is obviously irrelevant, then:

    i) a high card indicates that West should continue the suit he led, hearts, i.e. East has the ♥K;

    ii) a low card indicates the desire for a switch, as in the above hand. Thus the ♦2 would deny any further interest in hearts.

X-ray Eyes

We shall now consider more situations where the 'more haste, less speed' principle, discussed in the first chapter, is applicable and where communication, this time in the form of an exchange of information, is also necessary.

To rush is not to crush!

Do not commit yourself to a particular line of defence when you have the opportunity to wait for a more information, notably by a signal from partner. This is likely to apply in situations when you need to get partner in, typically for a ruff or a lead through a tenace, and are in a position to wait for the vital clue:

Dealer North				**North**
E-W vulnerable				♠ 10 6 5

W	N	E	S
pass	3♦[1]	pass	4♥

[1] shows a heart pre-empt

North
♠ 10 6 5
♥ Q J 8 6 5 3 2
♦ J 7
♣ 8

West
♠ K 8 3
♥ A 10 4
♦ 3
♣ K 10 7 5 4 2

You lead the ♦3 to the ♦7, ♦8 and ♦Q. Declarer plays the ♥K. How do you defend?

To be realistic, you are likely to defeat this contract only if you can get partner in to give you your diamond ruff, implying that he must have one of the black aces; but which? At present, it could be either but you can easily afford to duck one round of trumps, confident that partner will show out on the second (or else declarer will need to play a black suit to reach dummy, revealing all). Partner will then have the opportunity to signal.

North
♠ 10 6 5
♥ Q J 8 6 5 3 2
♦ J 7
♣ 8

West
♠ K 8 3
♥ A 10 4
♦ 3
♣ K 10 7 5 4 2

East
♠ A J 7 2
♥ 9
♦ K 10 9 8 5
♣ J 6 3

South
♠ Q 9 4
♥ K 7
♦ A Q 6 4 2
♣ A Q 9

Here, he will throw an encouraging spade and you will take four tricks. You should only take full credit, however, if you played the ♥10 under the ♥K, indicating a wish to ruff.

Points to remember

1. When you are unsure which suit to lead and can wait for a signal without losing control, do so!

2. On the other side of the table, partner should seek every opportunity to give that signal. Here, it was easy because East had only a singleton heart. But suppose he had two and needed to give the signal by the second round. Normally, echoing in trumps indicates a desire to ruff and/or a trebleton where count is crucial. This is far too inflexible and should be extended to suit preference in situations like the above where trump count and desire to ruff are obviously inapplicable. When discussing signalling in my book on the subject, I pointed out that a very large number of defensive mishaps in the top-class game were due to failure to use suit-preference signals. Proficiency in this area is beyond price. This is an excellent lead-in to the next hand.

Take your chance in the wardrobe!

If declarer plays a suit in which your card is irrelevant, take the opportunity to signal suit preference. This is a simple example which is commonly mishandled.

Dealer South
Both vulnerable

W	N	E	S
			4♣[1]
pass	4♦[2]	pass	4♥

[1] Namyats, a strong 4♥
   opening
[2] relay to 4♥

North
♠ J 6 5
♥ Q 9 2
♦ Q J 10 3
♣ 10 7 5

West
♠ Q 9 3
♥ A 7 3
♦ A 6 5
♣ J 9 4 2

You lead the ♣2, to partner's ♣Q and South's ♣A. Declarer plays the ♦K which you win, partner following with the ♦9. How do you continue?

There was a case for your ducking the ♦K but, once you have won, there is little to be gained by partner's giving you the count. It is far more important for him to show you where his values are. Here the high diamond indicates the higher-ranking side-suit, spades, and you must switch accordingly to the ♠3.

North
♠ J 6 5
♥ Q 9 2
♦ Q J 10 3
♣ 10 7 5

West
♠ Q 9 3
♥ A 7 3
♦ A 6 5
♣ J 9 4 2

East
♠ K 10 7 2
♥ —
♦ 9 8 7 4 2
♣ Q 8 6 3

South
♠ A 8 4
♥ K J 10 8 6 5 4
♦ K
♣ A K

Two spade tricks are now set up to go with your two red aces. Failure to find an immediate spade switch allows declarer to attack trumps, eventually reaching dummy to discard his losers on the diamond honours.

We shall now replay that hand; this time, on trick two, partner follows with the ♦2:

North
♠ J 6 5
♥ Q 9 2
♦ Q J 10 3
♣ 10 7 5

West
♠ Q 9 3
♥ A 7 3
♦ A 6 5
♣ J 9 4 2

East
♠ 10 8 4 2
♥ 4
♦ 9 8 7 4 2
♣ K Q 8

South
♠ A K 7
♥ K J 10 8 6 5
♦ K
♣ A 6 3

Now you must persist with clubs; if you play a spade, declarer grate-
fully rises with the ♠J and discards his club losers on the diamonds
for eleven tricks.

Points to remember

1. Where declarer's suit is solid and the count is irrelevant, look for op-
    portunities to signal suit preference.
2. Remember that count is typically only given when it is necessary to ad-
    vise partner how long to hold up a control. In positions where, for ex-
    ample, dummy has plenty of entries, this is of little interest; suit
    preference should now probably take priority.

Beware of the stray bullet!

We now consider another position in which declarer is trying to
discard losers at an early stage. In a suit contract, if declarer cashes
a side-suit ace out of the blue and then turns his attention to another suit, it is likely that the ace was a singleton.

   This is a very simple example and yet one in which far too
many declarers would be allowed to get away with daylight rob-
bery:

Dealer East   **North**
E-W vulnerable   ♠ 8 7 4

W	N	E	S
		pass	1♥
pass	2♦	pass	2♥
pass	3♥	pass	4♥

North

♠ 8 7 4
♥ K J 2
♦ K Q J 7
♣ 5 4 3

West

♠ K J 10 6
♥ A 5
♦ 9 8 5 4
♣ Q J 10

You lead the ♣Q to the ♣3, ♣6 and ♣A. Declarer cashes the ♦A,
partner following with the ♦10, and continues with the ♥3. Quick!
How do you defend?

Did you play low nice and smoothly so that declarer has a guess on the queen of trumps? If you did, you have smoothly presented him with a hopeless contract! What was partner's ♦10 all about? Hardly a singleton as declarer would have no reason to play on his long suit before trumps were drawn. East could be starting a echo to show an even number but what is the relevance of the count in diamonds when dummy's holding is solid and you do not have the ace, so that you are not sitting there wondering how long to hold it up? No — partner has realised that the ♦A is a singleton and that South is trying to arrange quick discards before the lead is lost to your ♥A.

When we said 'Quick!', the hint was that you should play your ♥A quickly before something terrible happened. That ♦10 is clearly a suit-preference signal for the higher-ranking of the black suits, spades, and you should switch to a low spade and collect the three tricks which are rightly yours.

North
♠ 8 7 4
♥ K J 2
♦ K Q J 7
♣ 5 4 3

West
♠ K J 10 6
♥ A 5
♦ 9 8 5 4
♣ Q J 10

East
♠ A 9 2
♥ 9 4
♦ 10 6 3 2
♣ 9 8 7 6

South
♠ Q 5 3
♥ Q 10 8 7 6 3
♦ A
♣ A K 2

Points to remember

1)   If a declarer fails to draw trumps in situations where early ruffs in dummy or ruffing a long suit high are inappropriate, you have good reason to suspect that some sort of stealing is going on. Pounce before you get robbed.

2)   Notice partner's ♦10. On trick one, the ♣2 did not appear and his ♣6 could have been signalling encouragement in clubs. The ♦10 (which it costs nothing to play) confirms his preference for spades.

Losers — choose carefully!

Having seen the idea, try this next example:

Dealer West			
Neither vulnerable			

North
♠ 6 4 2
♥ A K 2
♦ Q J 10 9
♣ 6 5 4

W	N	E	S
pass	pass	pass	1♥
pass	3♦¹	pass	4♥

¹ heart raise with ♦ **values**

East
♠ A 8 7
♥ 6 5
♦ 8 6 4 3 2
♣ 9 8 7

Partner leads the ♣Q to the ♣4, ♣7 and ♣A. On the ♦A, partner plays the ♦7. All follow to a heart to the ♥A and declarer plays the ♦Q, discarding the ♣2. Partner wins with the ♦K and plays the ♠9, which you win, as declarer follows with the ♠3. How do you continue?

You can see that there are two high diamonds waiting in dummy and that you must defeat the contract now or never. Declarer obviously has the ♣K and your only hope is in spades. Partner's ♠9 looks like top of nothing and declarer seems to be bent on discarding club losers but continuing spades is your only hope.

North
♠ 6 4 2
♥ A K 2
♦ Q J 10 9
♣ 6 5 4

West
♠ K J 9
♥ 9 7 4
♦ K 7 5
♣ Q J 10 3

East
♠ A 8 7
♥ 6 5
♦ 8 6 4 3 2
♣ 9 8 7

South
♠ Q 10 5 3
♥ Q J 10 8 3
♦ A
♣ A K 2

Now, which card did you play under that ♦A? It should have been the ♦8! Your ♣7 on trick one could well have been misread for an encouraging card with fatal consequences.

Points to remember

1. Note again the near certainty that the ♦A is singleton. Otherwise, why did South not attempt the finesse? If he started with ♦A K doubleton, and was beginning to unblock before taking discards, your carding, at least as far as the count of the suit is concerned, is of no interest. Suit preference, however, is likely to be crucial.

2. Did you notice partner's ♦7, the higher of his two low cards, also trying to indicate an interest in spades? Get into the habit of looking for these suit-preference signal opportunities; they save countless defensive errors.

3

First Impressions

We have all been reminded many times that trick one is often a critical moment for declarer, when contracts are won and lost. This is equally true for the defenders.

The head of the queue shows the door!

When defenders are likely to want to attack a suit, the partner of the potential leader should, if possible, give an indication of his strength. When you have a sequence in a long suit and a very weak hand, discard the top card to indicate your holding. This situation is likely to occur when your partner needs to get you in for a ruff or a lead through a tenace position.

Dealer South				**North**
Neither vulnerable				♠ K Q 7 6

W	**N**	**E**	**S**
			1♠
dbl	2NT[1]	pass	4♠

[1] limit raise of spades

North
♠ K Q 7 6
♥ 10 7 6 4
♦ 7 4
♣ A 6 3

East
♠ 8 4
♥ Q J 3
♦ J 10 9 8 2
♣ 10 7 2

Partner leads the ♥A. Which card do you play?

In this position, it is likely that West will want at least one minor-suit lead from your sid. He might well have ♦AQ or ♣KJ, holdings which he cannot profitably touch from his side. You should reasonably assume that partner has the ♥K and that an underlead at trick two will get you in. You should indicate this with the ♥Q on trick one.

Partner can now find the only defence to defeat the game by underleading his heart honour at trick two, after which a diamond from you will net two more defensive tricks. On any other defence, declarer has time to discard a diamond loser on his long club.

North
♠ K Q 7 6
♥ 10 7 6 4
♦ 7 4
♣ A 6 3

West
♠ 5 3
♥ A K 9 2
♦ A Q 6 3
♣ 9 5 4

East
♠ 8 4
♥ Q J 3
♦ J 10 9 8 2
♣ 10 7 2

South
♠ A J 10 9 2
♥ 8 5
♦ K 5
♣ K Q J 8

Points to remember

1. Look for every possible opportunity to indicate solid holdings of this kind, notably where you have a very weak hand and are unlikely to be able to win a trick in any other suit.

2. When partner plays his second heart to put you in, he should try to play a high heart to indicate a preference for the higher of the two remaining suits and vice versa in accordance with normal suit-preference style. In this case, he would lead the ♥9 to indicate his desire for a diamond through.

Underleading knows no bounds!

Having seen the idea, you can try this next example:

					North
Dealer East					♠ 10 9 7 4
N-S vulnerable					♥ A 6 5

W	N	E	S
		pass	1♦
2♣	dbl[1]	4♣	4♥
5♣	5♦		

¹ negative

North
♠ 10 9 7 4
♥ A 6 5
♦ K 9 8 5
♣ 5 2

West
♠ 3
♥ 10 8 3 2
♦ A 6 3
♣ A K Q 6 4

First of all, what do you lead?

The best way to approach this problem is to consider where your three tricks are coming from. If there is a void in clubs against you, there is probably no hope and, indeed, opponents may well have missed a slam. At the other extreme, it is unlikely that both opponents will be able to follow clubs twice so you should work on the assumption that exactly one round will stand up. Give partner the ♣J and you can see that you have an entry to organise a spade ruff. You should therefore lead the ♠3.

This runs to the ♠10, ♠2 and ♠A and South continues with the ♦Q. How do you defend?

Here there is no rush. You have three trumps and can hold up for one round without losing the chance of a ruff. So you duck and partner follows with the ♦2. On the ♦J, you win and partner discards the ♣J. How do you continue now and would it make any difference if partner discarded the ♣10? As a third alternative, how would you defend if partner discarded the ♣9?

In the first case, your dream has come true and you can underlead your club honours for a spade ruff. In the second case, partner has promised the ♣9 but denied the ♣J. Now you have no alternative but to try clubs from the top, hoping that South has a doubleton after all.

These two situations have been discussed many times. What has not been so carefully considered is the position where partner has ♣J 9 x x and South has the ♣10. Now East cannot afford the ♣J for obvious reasons and his ♣9 could also be from ♣9 8 x x.

North
♠ 10 9 7 4
♥ A 6 5
♦ K 9 8 5
♣ 5 2

West
♠ 3
♥ 10 8 3 2
♦ A 6 3
♣ A K Q 6 4

East
♠ J 8 6 5 2
♥ J 7
♦ 2
♣ J 10 9 7 3

South
♠ A K Q
♥ K Q 9 4
♦ Q J 10 7 4
♣ 8

Points to remember

1. Note that East played low at trick one. He could see that your lead could only be a singleton; 'third-hand-high', and 'cover an honour' are both inapplicable here.

2. Observe the duck by West at trick two, which can hardly cost, so that he earned the opportunity to see his partner's signal.

3. Think about the discussion on East's discarding in clubs to indicate his holding.

Rising betrays solidity!

Many contracts are thrown at declarer through defenders' failing to draw inferences from the way declarer plays a hand, notably his first card from dummy. If declarer rises with an honour in dummy at trick one, he will almost certainly be solid in his hand; roll-call his cards accordingly.

Few declarers are so kind (or masochistic!) as to refuse a free finesse if one is offered. Therefore, if a declarer plays in such a co-operative manner, you have every good reason to be suspicious as in this example:

Dealer East
N-S vulnerable

W	N	E	S
		pass	1♣
pass	1♦	pass	2NT
pass	3NT		

North
♠ A 9 5
♥ 10 9 5
♦ Q 8 3 2
♣ A 8 5

East
♠ 10 6
♥ Q J 7 4 2
♦ J 10 7 5
♣ K 7

Partner leads the ♠4 to dummy's ace, South playing the ♠3. A low diamond to the ♦A and West's ♦6 is followed by the ♣Q, run to your ♣K, partner playing the ♣4. What do you play next?

That ♠A is very revealing. If declarer had the ♠Q but not the ♠K, he would hardly have risen with the ♠A. Equally, if he had the ♠K J without the ♠Q, or the ♠J without the ♠K and ♠Q, he would have played low. Clearly he is not frightened of spades and is trying to conceal his strength in that suit. It must, therefore, be right to switch and your obvious hope lies in hearts. You should return a low heart as leading the ♥Q will promote dummy's ♥10.

If declarer has the ♥K doubleton, he is likely to go wrong now. Admittedly, he can make the contract by playing low but that offers only the 25% chance of your holding both ♥Q and ♥J. Rising with the ♥K, playing you for the ♥A, is obviously twice as good. In practice, he will finish two tricks short.

North
♠ A 9 5
♥ 10 9 5
♦ Q 8 3 2
♣ A 8 5

West
♠ J 8 7 4 2
♥ A 8 3
♦ 9 6
♣ 9 6 4

East
♠ 10 6
♥ Q J 7 4 2
♦ J 10 7 5
♣ K 7

South
♠ K Q 3
♥ K 6
♦ A K 4
♣ Q J 10 3 2

Points to remember

1. Notice declarer's play. Had he played low and won the first trick in hand, the ♠A would have remained in dummy as a visible second stopper. The heart switch would now have been far more obvious.

2. When declarer plays in this manner, tenace positions can usually be safely ruled out. This is helpful in placing honour cards.

4

The Crystal Ball

We shall end this lengthy chapter with a look at positions where defenders need to anticipate declarer's line of play. The bidding is likely to be a mine of information in this area.

If you've got it, use it!

If it is clear that defenders have the side suits well controlled, draw trumps. We shall start with a very simple example:

Dealer South
N-S vulnerable

W	N	E	S
			1♠
1NT	2♠	3♥	4♠

North
♠ Q 9 2
♥ K J 8 3
♦ 8 7 5 4 3
♣ 6

West
♠ A J
♥ 4 2
♦ A K J 10 2
♣ K J 9 3

You lead the ♦A to the ♦3, ♦Q from partner and ♦6 from South. How do you continue?

Partner should hold a good heart suit to have competed at the three-level. You are well endowed in both minors. Clearly, if South is to come near this game, he will have to ruff clubs in dummy.

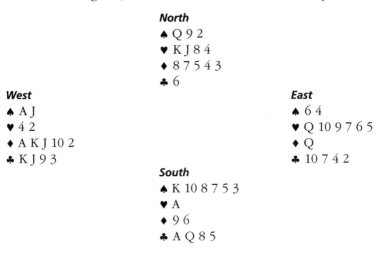

North
- ♠ Q 9 2
- ♥ K J 8 4
- ♦ 8 7 5 4 3
- ♣ 6

West
- ♠ A J
- ♥ 4 2
- ♦ A K J 10 2
- ♣ K J 9 3

East
- ♠ 6 4
- ♥ Q 10 9 7 6 5
- ♦ Q
- ♣ 10 7 4 2

South
- ♠ K 10 8 7 5 3
- ♥ A
- ♦ 9 6
- ♣ A Q 8 5

This plan should, at least, be restricted to only partial success by an immediate trump switch, ace and another.

Points to remember

1. It is likely to be safe to cash a second diamond before the trump switch, partner being unlikely to toss in the ♦Q from a doubleton, but did you notice that an immediate trump switch does not cost? That is in spite of the fact that you now lose your second top diamond, declarer being able to discard it on the ♥K. But now he loses three club tricks — one down. If you cash the ♦K before the trump switch, he discards a club loser on the ♥K instead; still one down — no difference.

2. This kind of situation often occurs when you have two good side suits and partner has bid the third. A trump lead is then called for, even if it has to be from an embarrassing holding like Q 7 5. The trick lost by virtue of the free finesse will often come back, possibly with interest. At worst, you will usually break even.

Obviousness is always the enemy of correctness

Try the following opening lead problem:

Dealer East					**West**
Neither vulnerable					♠ 9 5 2

W	*N*	*E*	*S*
		3♥	pass
pass	dbl	pass	4♠

West

♠ 9 5 2
♥ 5
♦ A K 9 7 3
♣ A K 10 8

What do you lead?

A heart lead seems obvious and unlikely to do much harm. But it is clear that, if this contract is to be made, many trump tricks will be needed. To prevent this, a trump lead is best. Side-suit tricks are unlikely to run away.

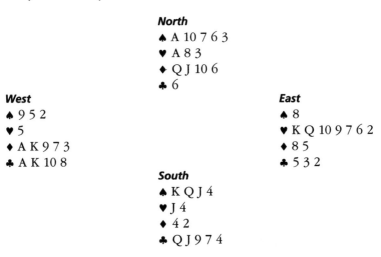

North
♠ A 10 7 6 3
♥ A 8 3
♦ Q J 10 6
♣ 6

West
♠ 9 5 2
♥ 5
♦ A K 9 7 3
♣ A K 10 8

East
♠ 8
♥ K Q 10 9 7 6 2
♦ 8 5
♣ 5 3 2

South
♠ K Q J 4
♥ J 4
♦ 4 2
♣ Q J 9 7 4

What you should avoid is trying to cash your minor-suit tops. You might hit the wrong one. When a similar hand appeared in a top-class international match, West led the ♣A, allowing South to ruff out the ♣K and establish a trick in the suit to make the contract with five spade tricks, a ruff, two diamonds, the ♥A and the club.

Points to remember

1. Note that side-suit tricks are unlikely to be lost in this kind of situation. There is no rush to cash them and you might well help declarer if you do.

2. Even if partner has the ♥A and a heart lead would result in an immediate ruff, you would probably at least still break even with the trump lead. The chance of a ruff has not been lost and, if South is to prevent it, he will have to draw three rounds of trumps, reducing his ruffing power markedly. In that event, where are his tricks to come from?

4

Trouble With Trumps

From reducing declarer's ruffing power, we turn to the converse, increasing that of the defenders. Far too many defenders, looking at poor trumps, give up hope too easily, unaware that an attack on declarer's resources could lead to unexpected trump tricks for their side. In this section, we shall look at the different ways of producing defensive trump tricks.

Enemy guns may prove to be their weakness!

If there is obviously no hope in the side suits, consider that declarer may be weak in trumps and attack accordingly. Beginners are usually taught that giving away a ruff and discard is one of the worst offences that a defender can commit. Against that, if declarer has no losers to ruff, and particularly if his trump holding is less than solid, a ruff and discard is probably going to be the last thing he wants.

Dealer South
E-W vulnerable

W	N	E	S
			3♦
pass	3♥	pass	4♦
pass	5♦		

North
♠ 6 4
♥ A K J 10 2
♦ K 6
♣ A Q J 10

East
♠ A 9 8 7 5 3 2
♥ 6 5
♦ 10 5
♣ 9 4

Partner leads the ♠K to the ♠4, ♠9 and ♠J. On the ♠Q, dummy following, how do you defend?

This is a typical position where it is obvious that, regardless of who has the ♣K or ♥Q, the defence has no hope in either suit. The only chance lies in trumps. Giving South seven cards for his pre-empt (notwithstanding that nowadays, particularly at this vulnerability, anything goes!) leaves two for partner and, if they are the ♦Q J, there is hope for your ♦10.

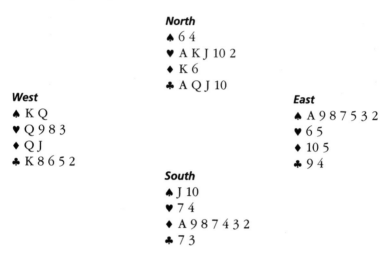

North
♠ 6 4
♥ A K J 10 2
♦ K 6
♣ A Q J 10

West
♠ K Q
♥ Q 9 8 3
♦ Q J
♣ K 8 6 5 2

East
♠ A 9 8 7 5 3 2
♥ 6 5
♦ 10 5
♣ 9 4

South
♠ J 10
♥ 7 4
♦ A 9 8 7 4 3 2
♣ 7 3

You should therefore overtake the spade, hoping that South can still follow (if he cannot, you have no chance anyway and nothing is lost), and lead a third round of spades. Partner ruffs to knock out or *uppercut* dummy's ♦K and you suddenly have a setting trick.

Points to remember
1. Giving a ruff and discard is only likely to cost when declarer has losers to discard. If he hasn't, he is unlikely to derive any benefit.
2. When declarer's trumps are likely to be his weakness, a forcing game is often in order even if he has the choice of where to ruff.

Diamonds are forever!

Having seen the idea, we can extend it to a more complex example where we shall see that one ruff and discard may not be enough. Remember, James Bond was supposed to be a keen bridge player!

Dealer South
E-W vulnerable

W	N	E	S
			1♥
2♦	dbl[1]	4♦	pass
pass	4♥	pass	pass
dbl			

[1] negative

North
♠ K Q 10 5
♥ A 10 5
♦ J
♣ K Q 10 5 2

West
♠ 9 7
♥ K Q J 2
♦ A 10 9 7 6
♣ 8 3

You lead the ♦A to the ♦J, ♦5 and ♦K. How do you continue?

You are disappointed to see the ♥A and a singleton diamond appear in dummy, but you will still certainly make two trump tricks and the ♦A. It is obvious that there is no future in either black suit and your only hope for a fourth trick lies in trumps. To achieve this, a full-scale onslaught on declarer's trumps is necessary. Simply continue diamonds now and every time you get in with trumps. Irrespective of where declarer ruffs, you cannot be denied a third trump trick.

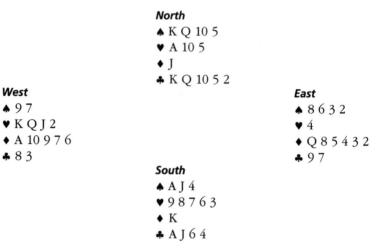

North
♠ K Q 10 5
♥ A 10 5
♦ J
♣ K Q 10 5 2

West
♠ 9 7
♥ K Q J 2
♦ A 10 9 7 6
♣ 8 3

East
♠ 8 6 3 2
♥ 4
♦ Q 8 5 4 3 2
♣ 9 7

South
♠ A J 4
♥ 9 8 7 6 3
♦ K
♣ A J 6 4

On any other defence, declarer is a move ahead.

Points to remember

1.   There are situations where you have to give a ruff and discard every time you get in. Here, three are needed.
2.   Note that, if declarer tries to minimise the effect of the forcing defence by ruffing early in dummy, he still goes down. If he leads the ♥10 from dummy in an attempt to duck the first round of trumps, you win and return the ♥2 to the ace, to leave your remaining two honours as winners. If he returns to hand and plays a trump towards dummy, you split your honours, win the next round and keep playing diamonds. Eventually, your ♥2 will score!

Gun for promotion!

We shall now consider other ways of promoting trump tricks. If you have poor trumps, do not give up hope; aim to shift the hierarchy. There are several ways of doing this and, as countless points are thrown away through failure to realise defensive trump tricks, it will be worth spending some time to work on recognising the various situations.

This first example illustrates several points:

Dealer East				**North**
Both vulnerable				♠ 6
W	**N**	**E**	**S**	♥ J 7 3
		pass	1♥	♦ K J 8 3
pass	2♥	pass	4♥	♣ Q 8 6 4 2

East
♠ J 10 9 5 2
♥ 10 5
♦ 9 6 4 2
♣ A K

Partner leads the ♣J, dummy plays low and you win as South follows with the ♣3. How are you going to defend?

There is a possibility of getting a club ruff and, even if South is able to overruff, you may be able to dislodge a high honour from South's hand (again an *uppercut*) to promote a trump trick in your partner's. Thus your first duty is to clarify your doubleton holding to partner by winning your tricks in the unusual order — the first with the ♣A and the second with the ♣K .

South follows with the ♣7 and partner with the ♣10. What do you play next and would it make any difference had partner's second club been the ♣5?

Having been told about your doubleton, partner's duty is to signal his entry. A high club thus indicates spades and and a low one, diamonds. So after the ♣10, you return a spade, but after the ♣5 you would return a diamond. Partner wins with the ♠A, and on the ♣9, dummy plays low; which card do you play?

Here you must hit it as hard as possible with the ♥10. That card has no hope of a trick in its own right but it could force an honour from South:

North
♠ 6
♥ J 7 3
♦ K J 8 3
♣ Q 8 6 4 2

West		**East**
♠ A Q 7 4		♠ J 10 9 5 2
♥ Q 2		♥ 10 5
♦ 10 7 5		♦ 9 6 4 2
♣ J 10 9 5		♣ A K

South
♠ K 8 3
♥ A K 9 8 6 4
♦ A Q
♣ 7 3

South must overruff and now nothing can prevent a fourth defensive trick for the ♥Q.

Points to remember

1. Dummy played low on trick one; covering the ♣J can never be right
2. East plays his honours in the 'wrong' order to indicate the doubleton.
3. West, when told that a ruff is on, must signal his entry with a suit-preference signal.
4. East should ruff as high as possible to try to promote his partner's trumps.

Voids preclude finessing!

Another way to promote a trump trick is to force declarer's or dummy's hand to ruff so often that it cannot take finesses.

				North
Dealer East				♠ A K J 6
Neither vulnerable				♥ 8
W	**N**	**E**	**S**	♦ A 9 4
		pass	2♦[1]	♣ J 10 7 5 3
pass	5♦			

[1] weak

East
♠ Q 10 4 2
♥ 7 5 3
♦ J 5 3
♣ A K Q

As you see, North has taken a very rosy view of his hand! Partner leads the ♥K, won by South. Declarer then plays the ♣8, partner following with the ♣2; you win perforce. How do you continue?

You have nothing in hearts and there is scarcely more hope in
spades. You can see that the clubs are breaking favourably for declarer. It appears you have two club tricks, but the only hope for
more is in trumps. If partner has the ♦K, again, your line of defence is likely to be irrelevant. The critical case arises when partner's
singleton is the ♦Q. Now, if you exit in trumps, in an attempt to re-
strict heart ruffs, declarer might get home if he wins the first round
the ♦A from dummy and continues clubs. Having seeing your partner's ♦Q, he may finesse against your ♦J, and use the two spade entries to ruff out clubs, on which he will discard his two heart losers.

North
♠ A K J 6
♥ 8
♦ A 9 4
♣ J 10 7 5 3

West
♠ 8 5 3
♥ K Q 10 9 4 2
♦ Q
♣ 9 4 2

East
♠ Q 10 4 2
♥ 7 5 3
♦ J 5 3
♣ A K Q

South
♠ 9 7
♥ A J 6
♦ K 10 8 7 6 2
♣ 8 6

To foil this plan, you must continue hearts, forcing dummy to ruff.
On winning your second club trick, a third round of hearts will
leave dummy with a singleton ♦A and your ♦J cannot now be
caught.

Points to remember

1. On seeing a side-suit singleton in dummy, many players switch to trumps
    without giving the matter a second thought. This is often correct but
    when it is clear that a) declarer is trying to set up another side-suit, b) that
    side-suit is breaking favourably for him, and c) there are entries in dummy
    to cash that side-suit, then, by drawing trumps, you are more likely to be
    helping declarer. In these cases, forcing dummy may well be the correct
    defence.

2. Note the need for East to make assumptions regarding his partner's
    trump holding which are consistent with the bidding and also sufficient
    to defeat the contract.

Ruff and sluff may be lethal stuff!

In order to gain a trump promotion, it is sometimes necessary to give a ruff and discard but, as we learnt earlier, when declarer has no losers to discard, this is very often a tasty but fatal medicine.

				North
Dealer East				♠ A K Q 4
Neither vulnerable				♥ K Q 9 8 6

W	N	E	S
		pass	pass
1♣	dbl	pass	1♥
2♣	4♥		

Dealer East
Neither vulnerable

North
♠ A K Q 4
♥ K Q 9 8 6
♦ Q J 7
♣ A

West
♠ J 6
♥ A 7
♦ A K 10 6
♣ Q J 10 7 2

You lead the ♦A to the ♦7, ♦2 and ♦4. How do you continue?

It is clear that you are not going to get rich on either black suit. Assuming partner's ♦2 indicates a trebleton, you have three tricks in the reds but where is the fourth? The only realistic hope is in trumps, where you'll need partner to hold the jack. Even if he does, it is likely to be part of a doubleton and a trump promotion is needed. You notice, with gratitude, that declarer may not be able to reach his hand easily and therefore may be unable to start trumps by leading low towards dummy's honours. That gives you a chance. Simply play the ♦K and a third round, locking declarer in dummy. If South has a singleton spade, there is nothing to be done. But if he has more, he will either have to start trumps with an honour from dummy or lead two top spades and ruff the third round. In either case, your ace of trumps will win and a fourth diamond will force dummy to ruff high, promoting partner's ♥J.

North
♠ A K Q 4
♥ K Q 9 8 6
♦ Q J 7
♣ A

West
♠ J 6
♥ A 7
♦ A K 10 6
♣ Q J 10 7 2

East
♠ 9 8 7 5 3
♥ J 2
♦ 5 3 2
♣ 9 6 5

South
♠ 10 2
♥ 10 5 4 3
♦ 9 8 4
♣ K 8 4 3

Points to remember

1. Notice the importance of the point that South has difficulty in reaching his hand. That represents the difference between success and failure in this contract. It has been noted before that it is a disadvantage to have the combined strength of the partnership concentrated on on side of the table; communication problems are now very likely.

2. Note that, if the positions of the ♦10 and ♦9 are exchanged, the contract is unbeatable. North unblocks his two honours in dummy on the first two diamonds, enabling him to win the third round in hand. Now a low trump towards dummy leaves the defenders helpless. Particularly in situations like this, where one hand of the partnership is very weak, it pays to be constantly on the look-out for these unblocking positions.

Allow yourself some help from partner!

Positions where one can promote a trump by refusing to overruff have been well documented. The following trump situations are common:

```
                  9 8 6 2
      A J                          7 3
                  K Q 10 5 4


                  9 8 6 3
      K 10 5                        7
                  A Q J 4 2
```

In each of the above trump positions, both South and West are now void in a side suit and East leads another round, South ruffing with the queen of trumps. Now, by refusing to overruff, West increases his trump tally by one trick. What he is effectively doing is forcing declarer to play a high trump on which he does not have to follow suit. Other positions are less obvious and a defender often needs to make assumptions regarding his partner's trump holding.

W	*N*	*E*	*S*
			1♥
pass	1NT	pass	4♥

Dealer South
Both vulnerable

North
♠ K Q 4
♥ 9 5
♦ K J 10
♣ 9 6 5 4 2

West
♠ 8 6 2
♥ K 7 4
♦ 9 8 6 5 3
♣ K Q

You lead the ♣K to the ♣2, ♣J and ♣3. Partner overtakes your ♣Q, South following with the ♣8, and plays the ♣7. South ruffs with the ♥Q. How do you defend?

If South's trumps are solid, you will make one trump trick, now or later, but no more. But give partner a couple of worthwhile trumps and refusing to overruff might be effective.

North
♠ K Q 4
♥ 9 5
♦ K J 10
♣ 9 6 5 4 2

West
♠ 8 6 2
♥ K 7 4
♦ 9 8 6 5 3
♣ K Q

East
♠ 10 7 5 3
♥ 10 8
♦ 7 4 2
♣ A J 10 7

South
♠ A J 9
♥ A Q J 6 3 2
♦ A Q
♣ 8 3

Just discard a spade or a diamond and re-examine the resulting trump position:

```
              9 5
    K 7 4                 10 8
            A J 6 3 2
```

Play as he might, declarer cannot avoid the loss of two trump tricks and the contract.

Points to remember

1. Unless there is a desperate rush to cash other top tricks quickly, it virtually never costs to refuse to overruff; it may well gain.

2. Note that, unless South ruffs high at trick three, he has no chance at all. When you are in a position to overruff, always think twice (and preferably well in advance — prior to the trick itself). If you can construct a holding for partner which could help to promote your trumps, be particularly reluctant to overruff, even with an honour which could be dropped otherwise.

To overruff may not be good enough!

Even experts go wrong in the following situation. Suppose the trump position on the last hand had been:

```
              6 5
Q 9                        K 7 4
           A J 10 8 3 2
```

Again, South and West are both exhausted of a side-suit, led by East. South ruffs with the jack. If West overruffs, he gives declarer a chance to pick up the trumps for no further loss with two finesses. If West refuses to overruff, there is no way for South to avoid the loss of two trump tricks. Note also that refusing to overruff, providing it is done smoothly, may well go unpunished, even when South has both ace and king. He will note that you 'could not' overruff and will probably play East for the queen, losing a trick anyway. You may have to be prepared to look silly occasionally when partner has exactly J 9 doubleton and declarer has ruffed with the ten, but faint heart never won fair lady! If you are not prepared to look silly occasionally, you are guaranteed a place half way down the field — no wooden spoon, but no prizes either!

Having seen the idea, try this next example:

Dealer North   **North**
Both vulnerable   ♠ 8 4
                        ♥ K 10 8
| W | N | E | S | ♦ A 6 4
|---|---|---|---| ♣ K Q J 10 6
| | 1♣ | pass | 1♥ |
| 2♠[1] | pass | pass | 3♥ | **East**
| pass | 4♥ | | | ♠ 7 3
[1] intermediate (11-14 pts.)   ♥ Q J 7 3
                                                      ♦ J 10 9 3 2
                                                      ♣ 5 2

Partner leads top spades, all following to two rounds. On the third round, dummy ruffs with the ♥8. How do you defend?

Clearly, South has the ♣A and there is little hope of defeating this contract without two trump tricks. South should be credited with a six-card trump suit. Thus, if you overruff now, the trump position will become clear when declarer starts to draw them with the ♥K and your remaining trumps will be picked up easily. But try the effect of discarding a club.

                          North
                          ♠ 8 4
                          ♥ K 10 8
                          ♦ A 6 4
                          ♣ K Q J 10 6
West   **East**
♠ A K Q J 10 6   ♠ 7 3
♥ —   ♥ Q J 7 3
♦ Q 7 5   ♦ J 10 9 3 2
♣ 9 8 4 3   ♣ 5 2
                          South
                          ♠ 9 5 2
                          ♥ A 9 6 5 4 2
                          ♦ K 8
                          ♣ A 7

This leaves the following trump position:

                          K 10
        —   Q J 7 3
                          A 9 6 5 4 2

Nothing now can prevent your taking two trump tricks.

Points to remember

1.   We saw earlier that it could be a mistake to overruff honours. Here even a card as low as the eight must be allowed to hold.
2.   In this case, the forced premature use of the ♥8 has promoted your ♥7 to make all the difference. But even if you only had the ♥6, there would still have been the small chance that partner had a singleton ♥9. Again, refusing to overruff can only gain and can rarely cost.

Eat first in haste — then digest at leisure!

We have seen situations where it is worth giving declarer a ruff and discard to weaken his trump holding. But where there is a danger that a ruff and discard will allow declarer to get rid of a loser, then defenders must be careful to cash their winners first:

Dealer South
E-W vulnerable

W	N	E	S
			1♥
pass	1NT	pass	3♥

North
♠ 7 5 2
♥ K
♦ J 10 9 7 3
♣ Q 8 7 5

East
♠ A J 10 3
♥ 9 8 6 4
♦ Q 6 2
♣ A J

Partner starts with the ♠K and ♠Q. You overtake and all follow to the third round. How do you continue?

You have a fourth trick in the ♣A but partner is unlikely to produce another high card. The only realistic hope lies in trumps but
partner is unlikely to have more than a singleton. If that should be
the ten or higher and dummy's king can be forced out, your nine
could be promoted. But you must cash the ♣A before playing a
fourth round of spades.

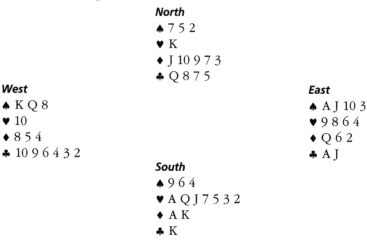

North
♠ 7 5 2
♥ K
♦ J 10 9 7 3
♣ Q 8 7 5

West
♠ K Q 8
♥ 10
♦ 8 5 4
♣ 10 9 6 4 3 2

East
♠ A J 10 3
♥ 9 8 6 4
♦ Q 6 2
♣ A J

South
♠ 9 6 4
♥ A Q J 7 5 3 2
♦ A K
♣ K

Observe the consequences of playing a fourth spade immediately.
South will merely discard his ♣K. He will accept the loss of a trump
trick but will still make his contract.

Points to remember
1. Note the loser-on-loser play by declarer if you give the ruff and discard
    too early. Even if the trumps were breaking 3-2 all the time, he will, at
    worst, break even.
2. The hand illustrates the importance of the defenders' cashing winners be-
    fore aiming for a trump promotion by giving a ruff and discard.

Dead honours are not lost causes!

Nevertheless, it is not necessarily vital for the defenders to cash out before engineering a trump promotion. What is vital is that declarer can only discard winners. Let's alter the previous hand a little:

North
♠ 7 5 2
♥ K 2
♦ J 10 9 7 3
♣ Q 8 5

West
♠ K Q 8
♥ 10
♦ K 8 5 4
♣ A 10 9 4 2

East
♠ A J 10 3
♥ 9 8 6 4
♦ Q 6 2
♣ 6 3

South
♠ 9 6 4
♥ A Q J 7 5 3
♦ A
♣ K J 7

The contract and first three tricks are the same. The difference is that, this time, East need not play a club which would put his partner on lead and spoil the trump promotion. On the fourth spade, South can discard a club but that is a winner rather than a loser. The ♣A does not run away as it would have done in the first layout. Having seen the idea, can you find the solution to the next problem?

Dealer South
Neither vulnerable

W	N	E	S
			1♠
pass	1NT	2♣	4♠

North
♠ A 6
♥ Q J 4
♦ J 10 9 7 3
♣ J 7 5

East
♠ Q
♥ 10 8 5
♦ A 8 5
♣ A K 10 8 6 4

Partner leads the ♣9 to the ♣5, your ♣K and South's ♣2. On the ♣A, South plays the ♣Q and partner the ♣3. How do you continue? Would it make any difference if the positions of the ♣J and ♣10 were exchanged?

After this auction, you cannot hope for partner to contribute very much but even a modest trump holding will suffice. You will obviously need to play a third club but first, you must cash your ♦A to guard against this likely situation:

North
♠ A 6
♥ Q J 4
♦ J 10 9 7 3
♣ J 7 5

West
♠ 10 9 4
♥ 9 7 3 2
♦ Q 6 4 2
♣ 9 3

East
♠ Q
♥ 10 8 5
♦ A 8 5
♣ A K 10 8 6 4

South
♠ K J 8 7 5 3 2
♥ A K 6
♦ K
♣ Q 2

On the third club, declarer can save himself from immediate disaster by ruffing with the ♠J but now nothing can prevent him from losing a trump trick by weight of high cards.

Points to remember

1. Despite the apparently unfavourable position of the ♠Q, partner needed very little in trumps to defeat the game.
2. If the ♣J is in your hand, you must still cash the ♦A. If you do not, South will discard the ♦K and, with dummy now out of clubs, a fourth round of the suit is less damaging. South discards and West, with the ♠A sitting over him, is helpless.

Discarding

In looking at discarding decisions, we now turn to another enormous source — probably the biggest — of defensive giveaways. Too many defenders lose interest when they are not blessed with their fair share of high cards; and yet it is often by holding on to the right low cards that the defence can be successful. But how do we know what to throw and what to keep?

Ignoring parity is declarer's charity!

If it is clear that declarer is going to play a specific number of rounds of a particular suit, it will usually right to keep the appropriate number of cards in that suit, *whether they are winners or losers.*

It is in this final italicised phrase that literally millions of points are thrown away all the time, and this especially applies to pairs' contests where careless discarding costs overtricks and, in consequence, matchpoints. For this reason, it is worth making a special effort to rectify failings in this area. It will be appropriate to start with a very extreme example to illustrate the point:

Dealer East
N-S vulnerable

W	N	E	S
		pass	1♣
pass	2♦	pass	2♥
pass	3♣	pass	3NT
pass	6NT		

North
♠ K 2
♥ 7 5
♦ A K Q J 10 6
♣ K J 10

East
♠ A 7 6
♥ J 10 9 2
♦ 5 4 3
♣ 4 3 2

Partner leads the ♠J to the ♠K and you win as South follows with the ♠3. You return the ♠7 and South wins with the ♠Q as partner follows with the ♠5. No need to tell you what is going to happen now — six rounds of diamonds. You can follow three times but will have to find three discards. What are they going to be?

Perhaps it would have been clearer had we asked what you are *not* going to discard. A huge majority of players would take one look at that dazzling club holding, and realising that the chance of winning a trick with it is considerably below that of seeing the Loch Ness Monster, they would discard clubs without giving the matter a second thought. The experts ask themselves *what is going to happen after the diamonds have been cashed.*

South almost certainly has a four-card club suit and will be looking to it for further tricks. If he has both the ♣A and the ♣Q there is nothing to discuss, but the critical case arises when he is missing the ♣Q. He has a two-way guess on the finesse and, if you discard the suit, you pin-point the ♣Q with partner.

So what would you discard? Count declarer's tricks — six diamonds and one spade; on the assumption above, there are two top club tricks to total nine so far. If South has ♥ A K Q, the hand is over without a club guess. What if he has the ♥A and ♥K only?

North
♠ K 2
♥ 7 5
♦ A K Q J 10 6
♣ K J 10

West
♠ J 10 8 5
♥ Q 6 3
♦ 8 7 2
♣ Q 8 7

East
♠ A 7 6
♥ J 10 9 2
♦ 5 4 3
♣ 4 3 2

South
♠ Q 9 4 3
♥ A K 8 4
♦ 9
♣ A 9 6 5

Now it is safe to discard your remaining spade and two hearts. If declarer keeps three clubs to keep a finesse option in both directions, partner will discard in the majors to keep parity with South. Declarer is then left with a guess in clubs.

Points to remember

1. Note the importance, particularly in high-level contracts, of counting declarer's tricks as a guide to placing outstanding high cards.

2. In this case, it seems ridiculous to discard from jack to four while keeping a hopeless trebleton. What you are actually doing is protecting partner's honour.

All generals were once privates!

This last hand was an excellent illustration of the importance of considering the partnership as opposed to the individual. If only people took this attitude in the world of marriage, wouldn't divorce rates drop through the floor?

Dealer East
Neither vulnerable

North
♠ J 6 5 2
♥ 7 4
♦ A Q 10 7
♣ A 4 2

W	N	E	S
		pass	1NT[1]
pass	2♣	pass	2♥
pass	2NT	pass	3NT

[1] 12-14 points

East
♠ K 7 4 3
♥ K 8 6 3
♦ 9 6 5 2
♣ 8

Partner leads the ♣J, which is won in dummy, South playing the ♣3. The ♥4 runs to the ♥3, ♥9 and partner's ♥10 and he persists with the ♣10. What do you discard?

The bidding and early play has clarified the heart position and it would clearly be folly to discard from your holding in that suit. What may be less obvious is that it would be just as ill-advised to discard a diamond. Declarer is going to play at least three rounds of the suit sooner or later and, especially as your highest diamond is higher than dummy's lowest, you must keep your full holding intact to ensure that declarer is restricted to his entitlement of three tricks.

North
♠ J 6 5 2
♥ 7 4
♦ A Q 10 7
♣ A 4 2

West
♠ Q 9 8
♥ Q 10 2
♦ K J
♣ J 10 9 7 5

East
♠ K 7 4 3
♥ K 8 6 3
♦ 9 6 5 2
♣ 8

South
♠ A 10
♥ A J 9 5
♦ 8 4 3
♣ K Q 6 3

The number of people who would discard a diamond, or even a heart, in this situation is alarming even if, to be realistic, the error will often go unpunished. Declarer will frequently have four diamond tricks by force anyway, holding either the king, or four to the jack.

Points to remember

1.   Even if declarer has four top (or easily establishable) diamond tricks, it will rarely cost to keep all four cards in the suit.

2.   If declarer has three spades (by no means ruled out on the bidding), and by discarding a spade, you allow him an extra trick in that suit, then it's likely that you never had a chance of beating the contract anyway.

Status may not echo importance!

It is the second point on the previous hand that is frequently missed. Players are very often frightened of discarding from holdings like Kx, Qxx, or Jxxx, fearing that their honour will be dropped as a result. Before hanging on to such holdings, you should be sure that declarer has all the higher honours (often he will not) and even if he has, that he also has the length and entries to take advantage of your discard.

For example, a declarer with Axx opposite KQx will gain nothing if you discard from jack to four! Even with KQ doubleton opposite Axxx, he will need an outside entry to the long suit. Notably in late stages of play, when tight discarding positions are most likely to occur, that entry may not be available. You can thus surely afford one discard and, if you are sure that partner has 10xx, you can afford more! Countless contracts and overtricks are thrown at declarer through errors in such situations.

Try this typical example:

Dealer East				**North**
Neither vulnerable				♠ J 5 3
W	*N*	*E*	*S*	♥ K J 8 3
		pass	1♠	♦ A K 8 7
pass	2♦	pass	3♠	♣ 9 4
pass	4♠	pass	5♣	
pass	5♦	pass	5♠	**East**
pass	6♠			♠ 7 4
				♥ Q 10 4
				♦ 10 9 6 3
				♣ 7 6 5 2

Partner leads the ♣Q, won by South's ♣A. Five rounds of trumps follow, partner following twice and then discarding the ♣3, ♣8, and ♣10. Now follows the ♣K from declarer, partner following with the ♣J. You have to find four discards, of which one will have to be red — which card?

You should have noticed that declarer showed no interest in trying to ruff clubs on the table and the subsequent play marked him with ♣A K doubleton. The bidding clarifies that he does not hold the ♥A and, if he did, the contract is cold anyway with six spades, three diamonds, two hearts, and two clubs for thirteen tricks. So partner has the ♥A and you must hope that he also has at least the jack and another diamond.

North
♠ J 5 3
♥ K J 8 3
♦ A K 8 7
♣ 9 4

West
♠ 9 2
♥ A 9 6 2
♦ J 4
♣ Q J 10 8 3

East
♠ 7 4
♥ Q 10 4
♦ 10 9 6 3
♣ 7 6 5 2

South
♠ A K Q 10 8 6
♥ 7 5
♦ Q 5 2
♣ A K

Counting declarer's tricks, you can see six spades, two clubs and three diamonds and, therefore, you must ensure that he does not make a fourth diamond by hanging on to your holding and discarding a heart. A 'canny' declarer may well now guess the heart wrongly on the basis that it is much easier for you to discard a low heart from ♥ A x x than from ♥ Q x x. In practice, with all the clubs gone, he will test the diamonds, and, if necessary, ruff the fourth round back to hand and try to guess the heart position at the end. With the actual hand, you might well try the deceptive discard of the ♥10, 'convincing' declarer that you do not have the ♥Q!

Points to remember

1. Note partner's club discards and that he hung on to hearts, trying to give the impression of holding three or four hearts to the queen.
2. Note the count on declarer's tricks helped you, yet again, to place the outstanding high cards and defend accordingly.

Never forget the auction!

Another position demanding parity arises when declarer appears to
be attempting to establish a suit. With countless trumps in dummy
ready to ruff your high cards, all seems lost but — hang on like
grim death!

Dealer South   **North**
Neither vulnerable   ♠ 8

W	N	E	S
			1♠
pass	1NT	pass	3♥
pass	4♦[1]	pass	6♥

[1] cue bid for hearts

North
♠ 8
♥ Q 10 8 7 2
♦ A J 2
♣ J 7 6 2

East
♠ J 10 6 5 4
♥ 9
♦ K 9 5 4
♣ A 10 5

Partner leads the ♣4 and your ♣A drops South's ♣K. It is obvious
that South is going to play on crossruff lines so you switch to your
trump, won by South's ♥A as partner follows with the ♥4. On the
♠A, partner plays the ♠3 and, on the ♠2, partner plays the ♠Q,
dummy ruffing. Declarer now plays a low trump from dummy.
What do you discard?

More accurately, the question should have been phrased: 'What do you *not* discard?' As long as you keep a doubleton diamond and all your spades, South is doomed by the bad spade split.

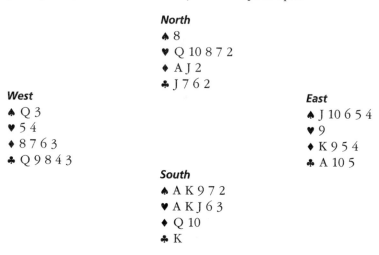

North
♠ 8
♥ Q 10 8 7 2
♦ A J 2
♣ J 7 6 2

West
♠ Q 3
♥ 5 4
♦ 8 7 6 3
♣ Q 9 8 4 3

East
♠ J 10 6 5 4
♥ 9
♦ K 9 5 4
♣ A 10 5

South
♠ A K 9 7 2
♥ A K J 6 3
♦ Q 10
♣ K

A spade discard allows him to ruff the suit high and a diamond will be discarded from dummy. Declarer's losing diamond can then be ruffed. Keep your whole spade holding intact and declarer is left at the mercy of the diamond finesse, failing as the cards lie.

Points to remember

1. It doesn't apply here but, if it came to choosing between discarding a spade and blanking the ♦K, the latter course is almost invariably right. As long as you do not think and squirm for a long time to give the show away, declarer, unaware of the position, is still likely to take the diamond finesse. Note that, following the discussion above, if partner has the ♦Q, it is perfectly safe to blank the ♦K in all circumstances.
2. The question arises as to whether you should have doubled 4♦ for the lead. I should recommend refraining from doing so. In this type of position, the information is more likely to benefit the enemy. In the deal above, you will have warned South that there is a certain diamond loser and, if he has the sense to take the hint, he will stop in 4♥ instead of bidding an unmakable slam. Even worse, with a singleton diamond and Kx in clubs, he may push on to a slam he would not otherwise have bid, confident that dummy will not include too much diamond wastage.

View the light at the end of the tunnel!

Countless points are thrown away all the time through poor discarding in the endgame. Many players find it difficult to remember every card that has been played and put that forward as their excuse when discarding wrongly at tricks eleven and twelve. But, very often, declarer's line of play will have given the show away even if you have forgotten. This is the type of position in which less experienced players continually falter:

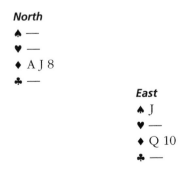

Dealer North				*North*
E-W vulnerable				♠ Q 7
W	**N**	**E**	**S**	♥ K Q 7
	1♦	pass	1♥	♦ A J 8 5 2
2♠¹	pass	pass	3♥	♣ J 7 6
pass	4♥			

¹ intermediate

East
♠ J 6 5
♥ 9 5
♦ Q 10 7 4 3
♣ 10 9 5

Partner cashes the two top spades, South following with the ♠2 and ♠9. Partner switches to the ♥J, won in dummy. The ♥K, all following, is followed by a club to the ♣K and partner's ♣A and West returns a club, won in dummy. All follow to a third round of clubs. Now South plays four more rounds of trumps, partner discarding four spades and dummy three low diamonds. As the last trump is played, this is what you can see:

North
♠ —
♥ —
♦ A J 8
♣ —

East
♠ J
♥ —
♦ Q 10
♣ —

Dummy discards the ♦8 as indicated above; what is your discard?

Even if you have forgotten what partner discarded, it should be clear that your correct discard is the ♠J. Actually, partner has thrown all his spades to indicate that he started with six and that South, therefore, had two. But even if he hadn't, if South held a third spade, he could have ruffed it early in the play to ensure an extra trump trick and the contract. As he didn't, he clearly was not interested in that ruff. He obviously started with a doubleton spade and the diamonds must be kept.

North
♠ Q 7
♥ K Q 7
♦ A J 8 5 2
♣ J 7 6

West   **East**
♠ A K 10 8 4 3   ♠ J 6 5
♥ J 8   ♥ 9 5
♦ K   ♦ Q 10 7 4 3
♣ A 8 4 3   ♣ 10 9 5

South
♠ 9 2
♥ A 10 6 4 3 2
♦ 9 6
♣ K Q 2

Points to remember

1. Declarer's refusal to ruff in dummy is frequently an indicator of his shape.
2. Note how West discarded a complete suit to help you count the hand. Where it is clear that a suit is out of the game (as is the case here in spades), get into the habit of discarding the whole lot if it will help partner with the count.
3. Of course, West could have made the position much clearer at trick three if he had switched to the ♦K but that could have been suicidal. Give South the ♦Q as a singleton or doubleton with weaker clubs, and such a play would merely be helping declarer set up his long suit. It is far better to attack dummy's entries — hence the trump switch.

The invisible is not exempt from the census!

In this next example, you have to visualise declarer's likely shape in order to keep parity. A top-class defender presented his opponents with a vulnerable game here. See whether you can do better:

Dealer South
Both vulnerable

W	N	E	S
			1NT[1]
pass	3NT		

[1] 15-17

North
- ♠ A 3
- ♥ Q 5 3
- ♦ 10 9 6 3
- ♣ Q J 10 7

East
- ♠ K 9 6 4 2
- ♥ 10 9 6 4
- ♦ 5 2
- ♣ 6 2

Partner leads the ♣4, dummy's ♣Q winning as you echo and South follows with the ♣5. The ♦10 is run to partner's ♦Q and West persists with the ♣3, won in hand with the ♣K. The ♦K from South is won by partner's ♦A and now he cashes the ♣A, South discarding the ♦4, and plays the ♣8, won in dummy. What are your two discards?

You can easily afford a spade on the first round but the second decision is less clear. Perhaps there are clues. Partner played the ♣8
from ♣9 8 on the fourth round of the suit, suggesting an interest in
the lower-ranking of the majors, hearts. Also count declarer's tricks.
He has three in clubs and will make two diamonds plus the ♠A to
total six so far. If he has both ♥A and ♥K to go with dummy's ♥Q,
the hand is over. The critical position arises here:

North
♠ A 3
♥ Q 5 3
♦ 10 9 6 3
♣ Q J 10 7

West
♠ 10 5
♥ K 8 2
♦ A Q 8
♣ A 9 8 4 3

East
♠ K 9 6 4 2
♥ 10 9 6 4
♦ 5 2
♣ 6 2

South
♠ Q J 8 7
♥ A J 7
♦ K J 7 4
♣ K 5

Now, if you discard a second spade, declarer can play on the suit for
two further tricks to go with the six detailed above. If he has the ♥A,
he is home. The safe discard is a heart.   It would be necessary to
keep the hearts if South had ♥ A K x x and partner ♥ J x but we
have established that the contract is then unbeatable.

Points to remember
1.   Note the suit-preference inference in partner's fourth club and the ne-
      cessity to count declarer's tricks on the various assumptions.
2.   After an auction in which South has bid spades, East would be far more
      likely to appreciate the danger. At the table, after the actual auction, a
      top expert did not — 700 points and 12 I.M.P.'s thrown away.

Conclusion

The number of situations covered in this book in which club and tournament players are error-prone is but a modest proportion of the whole spectrum. Nevertheless, if you have absorbed at least some of it, you will have taken a considerable step towards walking up to the rostrum and shaking hands in the prize-giving ceremony, rather than sitting among the applauding but disappointed losers. Success in this game is achieved not so much by brilliancies (although they always help!) but rather (as Chaucer emphasised in *The Nun's Story*) by eliminating your imperfections. Generosity to opponents may be appropriate in the bar but it is not so at the table and, with luck, the time you have spent with this book will have helped to keep this worthy asset in its rightful place

Other bridge titles from Master Point Press